HE CALLS ME LOVED

he calls me loved

A Study of Isaiah

HEIDI GOEHMANN

ilovemyshepherd

Unless otherwise indicated, all Scripture quotations are from the ESV® Bible (The Holy Bible, English Standard Version®), copyright © 2001 by Crossway, a publishing ministry of Good News Publishers. Used by permission. All rights reserved.

Please see a full list of references used in the back of this book.

Copyright © 2018 Heidi Goehmann

All rights reserved.

ISBN: 1986664201
ISBN-13: 978-1986664202

Introduction

Every year at the beginning of August, I do my yearly pep talk for myself.

> "This year is going to be great!"

> "I'll get up at 6am."

> "The kids will actually get out of bed before I threaten life and limb."

> "There will be hot breakfast. And freakishly healthy bento box lunches made with love and care by yours truly."

> "Instruments will be remembered. Folders checked with joy and zeal. Writing assignments completed with vigor."

> "My husband will be kissed before work and on his return home. Nothing will stand in the way of this goal, least of all small things, like preschoolers hanging off legs and pots boiling over."

> "There will be no yelling, particularly of the mom variety that scars small children for life."

> "No one will be rushing out the door with tears streaming down their face."

And my personal favorite…

> "I will do a daily devotion. This is happening, people. This is happening!"

It's like the start of a scholastic year gets in my blood and I think my sinner-saint self will magically manage all of life better with the introduction of tabbed folders and a new pack of washable markers.

It's a good thing. The breath of a new season in our lives is a great time to make some changes, adjust some habits…but I need real tools. And mostly I need some community. I need people to ask me, "How's that no yelling going?" and friends who will offer me forgiveness and mercy to help me dust myself off and keep on keeping on when I fall on my face.

I need someone to call me loved and redeemed on my good days and my worst days.

As I studied the Book of Isaiah, I found it is overflowing with God's realness, God's passion, and God's unrelenting affection for each of us. Throughout this Old Testament book, God speaks truth into our lives by sharing with us His vision of *who we are*. His vision is so very different from what the world tells us and even what we would tell ourselves.

The titles of affection and truth we find in Isaiah sustain us for the journey, and while they are perfect to discover in quiet study on our own, they come truly alive when we have one another — a group to gain insight with, ask hard questions, and shine mercy when life doesn't go as we planned.

Listen to these descriptors God proclaims over you:
- Loved
- Redeemed
- Holy
- Child
- Clay
- Ransomed
- Gathered
- Sought Out
- Awake

Discover these affectionate descriptions God showers on each of us, and more, as you turn the pages and study for yourself. He does call you loved…and so much more!

How to Use this Study

I Love My Shepherd strives to create resources that are easy to access and utilize, but also provide a consistent and thorough way to get into the Word every day. I Love My Shepherd studies are intensely theological, while being intensely practical, every time.

Each week, you can work through the Word in 3 ways:

Daily study readings:
He Calls Me Loved is an eight-week study. Each week, you will have the opportunity to work through various segments of the Book of Isaiah, alongside verses that interpret and connect for us throughout Scripture. There are five days of study to read each week. You can read it when and where you have the chance; if you miss a day of study in a week, not a big deal! Pick it up again, skip a day, or move to the next week. There is a whole lot of grace here. The goal is to *regularly* be in the Word, and that looks different for all of us.

Join or facilitate a small group:
Discussing the Word together gives us a firmer grasp on what God is speaking to us personally in that Word, as well as through one another's lives. Connection and community is a deep need God placed within each one of us. How we connect also looks different for each of us. Making a plan to discuss the Word over coffee with one friend, three friends, or making a formal study group with a set day and time, can bring the accountability we are looking for in our lives and a layer of enrichment and insight that can be surprising. You can also find video sessions to compliment this study on the I Love My Shepherd YouTube channel.

Scripture engagement and extras:

Drawing, taking notes, and journaling in the margins of this study book are welcomed and encouraged! Our brains are engaged more fully and for a longer period of time when we are given space for creative reflection. You will find visual faith tools for this study at ilovemyshepherd.com, under the Studies Available tab. You will also find I Love My Shepherd podcast episodes related to this study at ilovemyshepherd.com or wherever you get your podcasts. You will also find a weekly "heart verse" at the beginning of each week of study. This verse is a good one to write out each day in the margin, post somewhere on a sticky note, or memorize to internalize the truths God is proclaiming over you in this study.

I am so very thankful that you have chosen to invite me in and study the Word with me. I learn so much as I write each study, and especially when I hear from each of you! Do not hesitate to share your thoughts and insights with me by contacting me through the About Me page at ilovemyshepherd.com.

Happy studying, friends!

Love, Heidi ♡

he calls me loved

Isaiah 43:4a
Because you are precious in my eyes,
and honored, and I love you…

week one
He Calls Me Loved

You are Beloved
Three little words: Love and Doubt
The Story of Being Chosen
Love and the Removal of Shame
A Love that Overcomes

heart verse

Because you are precious in my eyes,
and honored, and I love you,
I give men in return for you,
peoples in exchange for your life.
Isaiah 43:4

he calls me loved
▼ ▼ ▼

day one
You are Beloved

The Bible is no ordinary book. It's quite amazing really. The Book of Hebrews, in the New Testament, describes it as living and active. It breathes life and salvation into a person. It moves in our lives every time we open it. Sometimes the message of eternity is so big, that we forget that eternity and its message are also for today. When we open the Bible, we can be assured that God has planned, from the creation of time, what we each need to hear for this particular day in front of us.

How is this even possible?! How does God take words, written in a book like Isaiah - a telling of and a message for a people so long ago - and make it profoundly meaningful for each one of us, walking around in the twenty-first century?

To that my short answer is – sit back and wonder for a moment — He is God.

This is who He is and what He does:

Father
Creator
Mighty
Lord
Savior
Redeemer
Listener
Leader
Restorer
Helper
Seeker

Isaiah is a book all about this God of ours. The titles above are just the beginning, and He calls us to hear, to give ear, for even just a minute in our day.

> *Hear, O heavens, and give ear, O earth;*
> *for the L*ORD *has spoken...*
> *Isaiah 1:2a*

One day I sat down and read the entire book of Isaiah from cover to cover in one sitting. I drank my coffee and was enraptured by the Word in an instant. I heard the story of a God who is zealous for His people. A God who has high expectations and lots of plans. A God who loves me so much that He was stricken and afflicted for my sake. Isaiah isn't just full of words *about* God, but words about *who God is*. It also shares God's vision for who we are, both without Him, and how much better we are with Him. This is just a snippet of what God says about us in Isaiah:

We are loved.
We are children.
We are neighbors.
We are holy.
We are righteous.
We are led.
We are saved.
We are consecrated.
We are strong.
We are upheld.
We are clay.
We are heard.
We are ransomed.
We are delivered.

Which of the above statements speak to you in your present relationship with God? Why?

This, my friends, is only one page. I have three more pages full to the brim and overflowing with titles and descriptions of our great God and His image, His forgiveness, reflected in a very much imperfect people. While we flip through the pages of Isaiah, we'll sort out who He is, related to my little life, in this place and this time on earth. We'll see how much God considers us in the big plan of eternity. As you turn your pages in the next eight weeks, *may you begin to see how much God thinks of you.*

We are never far outside His watch and His tender care.

Don't get me wrong, Isaiah will be hard. There will be plenty of words in our study like:
- desolation
- destruction
- brokenness
- blindness
- deafness
- forsaken
- hated
- and stubborn.

The imagery God utilizes through the prophet Isaiah is not sugar-coated. It is full of the hard truths of our own wantonness, our wanderings, our lustfulness, our true and broken reality. But, oh, the beauty of where this brings us in our relationship with Him!

From broken to restored,
lustful to holy,
wandering to found,
forsaken to gathered.

This is God's wild and wonderful love. Our God sent His only Son to walk among us. He raised Jesus up to raise us up. Through Christ, we are the people of God, and individual children of the Most High God.

You are beloved.

Exploration

For exploration today, as you prepare to study *beloved* this week, flip through the pages of your Bible. Turn to the Book of Isaiah in particular and jot down anything you find describing the life of the Israelites as the people of God throughout the book. How do these descriptions also apply to our lives as followers of Christ?

Or another option might be to take just one chapter from Isaiah of your own choosing and read through it, making notes on what God tells us about Himself in that one chapter and what He tells us about ourselves in that chapter as well.

If you're unsure where to go, find out more about the prophet Isaiah's calling and experience with the Lord's forgiveness in Isaiah 6. Answer these two questions as you read Isaiah 6:

What does God have to say about Himself?

What does God have to say about you?

he calls me loved
▼ ▼ ▼ ▼

day two
Three Little Words: Love and Doubt

About four years ago, I was sitting in my local women's Bible study, when the study author alighted on the Scripture in which our theme verse for the week rests, Isaiah 43. It's a beautiful passage. I'll highlight Isaiah 43:1-4 for you below, but if you have your Bible available, grab it out and read through the whole chapter for yourself. As you read, look for, and maybe circle or underline, the descriptions of God and the descriptions He gives to us as His people.

> *But now thus says the Lord,*
> *he who created you, O Jacob,*
>   *he who formed you, O Israel:*
> *"Fear not, for I have redeemed you;*
>   *I have called you by name, you are mine.*
> *When you pass through the waters, I will be with you;*
>   *and through the rivers, they shall not overwhelm you;*
> *when you walk through fire you shall not be burned,*
>   *and the flame shall not consume you.*

*For I am the L*ORD *your God,*
  the Holy One of Israel, your Savior.
I give Egypt as your ransom,
  Cush and Seba in exchange for you.
Because you are precious in my eyes,
  and honored, and I love you,
I give men in return for you,
  peoples in exchange for your life.

And that's only the first four verses, friends!

Isaiah is full of beautiful affection from our Lord to us. But the reason it captured my attention that day in Bible study so long ago, was those three little words...

I love you.

Read Isaiah 43:4 again and highlight those three little words in your Bible if you would. Write them on a sticky note or a piece of stationary. Write it on your child's backpack with a sharpie. Channel your inner fifth grader and write it on your hand with a blue ink pen. Write it somewhere and return to it again and again.

When I first found this verse in Bible study, all I could think was

> "Where has this verse been my whole life?"

and

> "How do all women not know about this?"

God's Bible is a love letter to us. Isaiah isn't the only book of the Bible that talks about His love. It's not even the only book that refers to His children as beloved — there's Deuteronomy, Hosea, Jeremiah, Romans, Corinthians, the letters of John, and more.

However, this is the only place I have ever found in the Bible that directly says *I love you*. Sometimes, we just need to hear it. We need to hear the three little words —

I love you — from God to us, direct, obvious, and to the point.

The problem is that all the stuff of life gets in the way — wars and health problems, finances and heartbreak, injustice across the globe and in our own churches and homes. With all the pain and heartache swirling around us, it can be hard to see love poured out by the Savior of the Nations.

This has been true throughout time. Open your Bible and read Hosea 2:16-23 to see how this was just as true in ancient Israel as it is for us today. Write Hosea 2:18 in the space below.

Hosea 2:18, which you just wrote out, assumes that we have been a people living outside of perfect. That we are a people in need of rescue from pain and struggle. It tells us that God sees, and He knows our doubt.

Compare Hosea 2:23 with Romans 9:25. What similarities and difference can you find?

We are very much loved. God, in Isaiah 43, tells us directly how much we are loved even when we wander away. It tells us that fire will come, waters will rage, life will be imperfect. God's love doesn't look like flowers and sunshine and roses of financial blessing pouring out of the sky. It doesn't look easy or pain-free.

Instead, it looks like relationship. It looks like a God who loves us through Christ, despite our frailness, despite our constant running off.

We are called beloved for one reason...because we are also called His.

We are His creation. We are redeemed We are His.

In His mercy, Romans tells us, which assumes we need mercy. We need mercy for our own failings, for the failings of the world around us. God gives us that mercy and then some. He also gives us Love.

It's so easy to doubt with the world looking suspiciously like it may cave in at any given moment. Just be honest with Him. Jesus knows our every weakness but proclaims His Word over us today and every day.

Rest in the mercy you find today in those three little words of Isaiah 43:4 -

I love you.

In your doubt and in your understanding, you are beloved.

Exploration

What things in the world are hardest for people to see God's love through, especially when they do not know Jesus?

When have you struggled with doubting God's love for you?

he calls me loved
▼ ▼ ▼

day three
The Story of Being Chosen

During our study, we will be all over the place in Isaiah. The book itself is not linear – that is, it's not chronological. Isaiah doesn't take us through a timeline of history like some books do. When you start at Isaiah Chapter One and read through, it's a beautiful book, but it won't go from A to B to C. My study Bible tells me that the Book of Isaiah covers at least 200 years of Old Testament History[i], circling in and around and back again on itself. The message of Isaiah isn't a narrative as much as it is a call and response of God to His people and the people to God. It is the message of Salvation played out again and again, preparing the way for Christ to come and save us, once and for all time.

Today, though, we are going to turn one page in our Bibles and go only as far as Isaiah 44.

Read Isaiah 44:1-5 below:

> "But now hear, O Jacob my servant,
>   Israel whom I have chosen!
> Thus says the Lord who made you,
>   who formed you from the womb and will help you:
> Fear not, O Jacob my servant,
>   Jeshurun whom I have chosen.
> For I will pour water on the thirsty land,
>   and streams on the dry ground;
> I will pour my Spirit upon your offspring,
>   and my blessing on your descendants.
> They shall spring up among the grass
>   like willows by flowing streams.
> This one will say, 'I am the Lord's,'
>   another will call on the name of Jacob,
> and another will write on his hand, 'The Lord's,'
>   and name himself by the name of Israel."

Part of the message of being loved is the message of being chosen.

Think of all the love stories you've watched play out on the screen. Girl loves boy. Boy isn't sure and is really preoccupied in life with something else. Girl does something or something happens to girl. Boy realizes he is missing out. Boy chooses girl. Love songs play and hearts take flight on the screen.

Or think of every young girl's longing for a best friend. Think of every middle schooler's desire to be picked, anything but last, in gym class. We want to be chosen. Being chosen is very often how we understand being loved.

Fill in Isaiah 44:1 below for a beautiful picture of God's love that *chooses* us —

"But now hear, O Jacob my servant,

Israel whom _____ _____

_____ !

What promise does 1 Peter 2:9-10 proclaim to Gentile believers of the New Covenant of Jesus Christ?

This may sound a familiar. The language is reminiscent of Hosea 2:23 and Romans 9:25, which we read in yesterday's lesson — *not a people, now a people; without mercy, now receiving mercy.* This is how God's Word works, ever weaving His love and promises into one another and into our lives.

What other promises can you find that speak of God's love and His choosing in Isaiah 44:1-5? Take a minute to jot down your own ideas in the margin before you go further. I'll list a few that I found also:

- We are formed lovingly by His hands.
- We are helped.
- Our fears are lifted.
- We have been filled.
- Our thirst for Life and goodness and mercy and justice has been quenched with the Spirit.

- We are blessed, our children are blessed. We know Christ in our lives and His forgiveness.
- We are raised up.
- His name is written on our hands. He claims us, choses us.

We are not drained. We are filled. How often have you been exhausted and need the promise of the Lord's love to fill you and sustain you? Weariness, you may come, but you may not reign in our lives.

We are *The Lord's!*

We are not forsaken. Our children are not forsaken. We are baptized believers of the Bright Morning Star. We rest in the promise of His salvation. His name is written on our forehead and our heart.

We are *The Lord's!*

We are not orphaned. We are greatly loved. We are made and formed by Him in the womb, planned before the dawn of time.

We are *The Lord's!*

Write it on your hand today, literally. Bring back fond adolescent memories by taking ink to skin. Write something more important than the homework due next Tuesday. Let your children and your friends ask about it. Write it large or write it in tiny script.

The Lord's!

This is your story of being chosen.

Exploration

Is there any time that you can recall when you felt left out or last to be chosen?

How does God choose His people differently than the world chooses people?

he calls me loved
▼▼▼

day four
Love and the Removal of Shame

How many relationships have you had in your life that made you feel loved? Not butterflies-in-your-stomach loved, but loved in a way that spoke safety into your life. Loved in a way that spoke care and concern. In this kind of safe love, you can be completely yourself, secure that even when you mess up, you will find forgiveness.

Name at least one relationship you have experienced with this kind of love. *If this exercise is hard for you, hold tight, there is hope in today's lesson.*

These relationships can be quite rare. They are most common in two particular places— with our parents and within marriage. If you aren't married, this kind of safe relationship might be something you dream about when imagining your future spouse – care, safety, acceptance. Very occasionally we find it in a true and wonderful friendship. This love is all the more special because it is rare.

In Isaiah 54, God uses language related to the relationships that generally make us feel safest in this life, so that we can begin to wrap our heads around the depth of His love for us. You'll hear words related to the roles of father, husband, wife, and mother.

God will always love us greater, stronger, more deeply and more faithfully than our parents or our spouse or our friends ever could. They are human and sinful. God is not. He is perfect. He is holy. His very name is Love. Fill in the missing words of 1 John 4:8 below, to see this truth in the Scriptures themselves.

Anyone who does not love does not know God, because

_____   _____   _____.

We need this kind of love in our life. The safest and most accepting love comes from God, through His forgiveness. Let's read Isaiah 54:4-8. As you read, notice the relationships God proclaims over his people. Look for those descriptor words, and titles for God, that speak of love and acceptance and safety. Jot them in the space here:

A little Bible backstory...

Israel, God's chosen people, had some issues. They had deserted their "marriage," or covenant, to the Triune God who loved them. They chased after other gods. These gods were as fake as a designer bag sold on a street in Queens. Ironically, these gods were not only useless, but also unsafe. They led the Israelites to adultery, orgies, violence, and child sacrifice. None of those have ever spoken safety into life. In the end, it led them only to shame. They were taken captive by the Babylonian empire, led into a new land, stripped ultimately of everything that spoke safety into their lives- their homes, families, land, and livelihoods, even while the Lord allowed them to escape with their lives.

Shame. It sits on our shoulders and rests heavy on our hearts. It eats at our stomach as a little parasite we call anxiety. We have been the deserter. We have walked away from the God who loves us for false security in any number of things. We have been cast off by the very things we chased after. Just like the Israelites, God allowed us to go and chase fruitless things. Read Isaiah 54:7 again. How long does God say he allows our chasing after things that would hurt us?

Essentially, He says to us – *I let you go your own way, because you were so determined.* Think of the safety in a relationship that doesn't hold you hostage, that doesn't say "You must walk this way, or else..." God loves us enough to let us walk down a deserted path. What promise is found in Isaiah 54:7?

Beloved, He's going to gather us up. During another week of study we'll talk about how He gathers His people together, but this week, think about the act of Love poured out from a God who gathers all of our individual broken pieces and puts them together again. Our God picks our shame-filled selves up off the floor and says,

Beloved, lift your head -
> *"Fear not, for you will not be ashamed; be not confounded, for you will not be disgraced..."*
>
> Isaiah 54:4

> *"...with everlasting love I will have compassion on you..."*

I am *"...your Redeemer."*

> Isaiah 54:8

This is all possible because that Redeemer offered His life for ours. Paul tells us the full story of Jesus offering His body to be "broken" on the cross for us, in 1 Corinthians 11:23-24:

> *For I received from the Lord what I also delivered to you, that the Lord Jesus on the night when he was betrayed took bread, and when he had given thanks, he broke it, and said, "This is my body which is for you. Do this in remembrance of me."*

His body, given for us, putting together our pieces, redeeming us, all of us, every part of us, head to toe and back again.

Whatever in your life you have done, wherever you have been, rest in the safe love of our God, who calls us back to Him.

Exploration

Which words or phrases from Isaiah 54 or any of the Scripture readings in today's lesson speak the truth of God's safe love into your life?

What do these say to you about the character of God?

he calls me loved
▼ ▼ ▼

day five
A Love that Overcomes

How many of us have seen an image or graphic with a lovely rainbow, stretched wide across the sky and its eloquent reminder that "God keeps His promises."

This connection is accurate. When we teach little children the story of Noah and the flood that covered the earth, at the end of the day, this is the message that we want them to get. God is faithful. God said He would save Noah, and He saved Noah. God said humanity would continue through the line of Noah and so here we are. God said He would never destroy the whole earth with a flood and so He will not. God does keep His promises.

However, Isaiah gives us the more grownup version of the story. And sometimes it's time to put on our big girl pants and read a little deeper, a little longer, a little harder.

Today, we'll return to Isaiah 54. Let's keep reading where we left off yesterday, beginning at Isaiah 54:8-12. As you read, note below any connection you find to the account of Noah and the ark.

How many of you have felt overwhelmed? I would brave a guess that at our house this is at least a once a week occurrence for me, and is probably more accurately acknowledged as once a day. In fact, if I'm honest, at any given time it's like a tape loop in my head. "I'm so overwhelmed. I'm so overwhelmed." So much to do and only so many hours in the day. There are tiny humans to keep alive. A husband to keep moderately happy at least. There are also so many needs around us everywhere. This is life. Life can be overwhelming.

Normally, when I address a topic like this I'd give you the 500 different reasons why you don't need to be overwhelmed. I'd share Bible passages about God being our rock, our hope, and our solid foundation. Today, though, when we read Isaiah 54, overwhelmed may be just the thing we need for a little while; not forever, not for good, but for a time.

Isaiah 54:8 proclaims,
> *"In overflowing anger for a moment I hid my face from you..."*

Anger is often overwhelming for us. It is a scary picture, the God of the Universe overflowing with anger. This idea stirs up all kinds of *overwhelming* for me. What have you been told or learned in your life about God and anger?

God's anger sits in a place of justice, but it also sits in a place of love.

A memory comes to mind of my mother when I was in my early twenties. My brother, 20 or so years my senior, was an alcoholic. In my effort to avoid labels I would say he had an unhealthy relationship with alcohol, and he would correct me. He had been sober for years and would honestly admit to friend and stranger alike, "I'm an alcoholic. Can't be around the stuff. I think it solves my problems and it never does." He was having a hard time and had come to stay with my parents. My brother was overwhelmed. He was overwhelmed by life and his pain. He was overwhelmed by his own inability to change and to change the world around him. One night he came home blindly drunk. I opened the door for him, and he fell flat on the ground.

The thing that sticks with me most in the memory is my mom's face. She was livid,

"Look at how far you've come, to throw it away! What happened? Why this? Why now?"

At the end of her rant, my father drew her into himself and not only her anger, but her love caused her next response...

She turned her face away. She could not look. It was too painful. She did not love my brother any less. I'm certain in that moment her heart was exploding with love for my brother, for each of us, for her family. She loved him so much that it hurt to look at the destruction.

God will not watch us destroy ourselves, but He also will not take over. He loves us enough to wait for the proper time, sometimes the bottom of the pit, to reach in and lift us up.

We find this truth in the account of Noah and the ark, referenced in Isaiah 54, found in its fullness in Genesis 6.

Read Genesis 6:5-8. Just how evil does the Scripture say people had become in Noah's time?

Think of how overwhelmed Noah must have felt, a believer of the Most High God, imperfect, but faithful, looking to Yahweh, through His strength alone. If you browse through Genesis 7-8, you will see that the promised flood did come. Noah's reality was not rainbows and sunshine for quite some time. Days and months of rain and flood lingered on.

How long did the flood last, according to Genesis 7:23-24?

150 days

Do you ever have a day when you hear one too many news reports and think, Lord have mercy!? Does the feeling of not being enough, not getting it right wash over you, flooding you...overwhelmed? Have you had a struggle in your family that causes you to look around and say, "I'm done, Lord. Overwhelmed. Finished. You take it from here." Read one very clear piece of the puzzle of all that is overwhelming in this life noted in the beginning of Isaiah 54:10:

> *For the mountains may depart*
> *and the hills be removed...*

We will be overwhelmed. The world is not getting better. Those mountains will depart the Scripture tells us. The hills will be removed. The original Hebrew language of this passage is active in nature. The Hebrew root for the verb *removed* in Isaiah 54:10 is *mot* which can also be translated as to shake, to slip, to fall, or to bring down[ii].

We will be shaken. We will fall. Difficult things will come. To add another layer onto that, when you love deeply, your family and your neighbors, as God intended, there will be days when the struggle washes over you and you feel a bit like you're drowning.

Here is the good news —

You may be overwhelmed, but you are not overcome.

Fill in the promises of God in Isaiah 54:10b below:

...but my __unfailing__ __love__

shall not depart from you,

and my __covenant__ __of__ __peace__

shall not be removed,"

*says the L*ORD*, who has compassion on you.*

This is the grown-up promise.

We may be overwhelmed, but we will not be overcome. God has made a covenant of peace with us in Christ Jesus. What title for Jesus is found at the very end of Isaiah 63:7-8?

__Savior__

We may be overwhelmed, but we are not overcome.

We have a Savior. His name is Jesus Christ, Savior of the World. He is not shaken. He is a solid foundation. He does not slip, even when the earth gives way.

God keeps His promises. We are not overcome.

Exploration
What things in your life at present leave you feeling overwhelmed?

How do you normally respond or cope with overwhelming news or emotions?

What difference can you see between *overwhelmed* and *overcome*?

Whether as an individual, or with your group, pray over one topic in the news currently that seems overwhelming.

he calls me ransomed

Isaiah 43:4a
Because you are precious in my eyes,
and honored, and I love you…

week two

He Calls Me Ransomed

No Longer Held Hostage
The Rescue of Ransom
The High Price of Ransom
All or Nothing Faith
The Ransom from Selfishness

heart verse

*And the ransomed of the L*ord *shall return*
and come to Zion with singing;
Everlasting joy shall be upon their heads;
they shall obtain gladness and joy,
and sorrow and sighing shall flee away.
Isaiah 35:10

he calls me ransomed
▼▼▼

day one
No Longer Held Hostage

Ransomed sounds like the name of a movie to me. I feel like it might be a good action movie, but maybe not. Maybe there would be more than adventure to the story. What would this movie be about? Take 30 seconds to let images come to your mind. Create tiny snippets of a screenplay and share your ideas here:

Biblically, the word *ransom* can get *really* interesting. Write Psalm 49:15 out in the space below and see just how interesting it gets.

> But God will redeem my life from the grave; he will surely take me to himself.

Sheol is the Hebrew understanding of the grave or the place where the dead reside, the underworld. Many commentators suggest the Greek equivalent of Sheol in the New Testament is Hades. That's just how interesting ransoming is Biblically.

Some Bibles translate the Hebrew word here as *redeem* in Psalm 49:15, while others use the word *ransom*. A minority of translations also use the word *rescue*. The same variance of word choices is also true for our theme verse this week, Isaiah 35:10:

> *And the ransomed [redeemed] of the L<small>ORD</small> shall return*
> *and come to Zion with singing;*
> *Everlasting joy shall be upon their heads;*
> *they shall obtain gladness and joy,*
> *and sorrow and sighing shall flee away.*

What do both *redeemed* and *ransom* have in common?

First, each word reflects payment associated with getting something back. They are both verbs, action words. They are about bringing someone back, making a situation right, ending captivity of some kind.

Let's look at another layer of these words...

What action is involved in the surrounding verses? This is one of the ways that translators make decisions of which English word would best express the original Hebrew intention. Turn to Isaiah 53. Feel free to read the chapter as a whole, but pay close attention to Isaiah 53:6-12 and write down any action words you find.

This is the language of ransom.

When I ponder the word *ransom,* images of kidnappings, hostage situations, and terrorism come to mind. These aren't pleasant thoughts, but they also are not Biblically far-off.

In ransoming someone, the emphasis is on bringing them out of something. The emphasis is on the action of the rescuer, the ransomer — going in, physically rescuing, delivering the thing, the people back to where or to Whom they belong. The action brings redemption. The main difference I could find between redeem and ransom however, is that in redeeming the emphasis is on the payment and in ransoming the emphasis is on *bringing someone out.*

There is a desperation to ransoming.

Someone needs to get out. We have to get them out now. Someone's very life is at stake.

One of the definitions of the Hebrew root word *padah,* for *ransom* or *redeem* in Isaiah 53:10, is related to using resources available - by any means, *any means.*

All of Isaiah 53 points us to Jesus Christ: Savior, Redeemer, Ransomer.

He was willing to bear the weight, to take any action necessary, to save us. He was willing to expend any resource at his disposable to rescue us, including His very life — for us, for you. Isaiah 53 lists the actions that would be required of Him. These words in Isaiah were written 800 years prior to His walk to the cross that would ransom each of our lives. That is both beautiful and remarkable.

The question left hanging though is,
"What does He ransom us from?"

We'll talk about this throughout the week. For our exploration today though, I've listed a few verses to wet your appetite. Look up each verse and note what insight it gives to the things that God the Father has sent Jesus to ransom us from. Remember that your Bible may say *redeemed* for any given verse. Read each passage using the word *ransomed* for our purposes today. As you look at each verse, write one word that stands out to you in the margin beside each reference. Then read my notes beside each for further reflection.

Hosea 13:14 – We are ransomed from death, violence, and our enemies. When the world rages, we know that we have been ransomed. We will not be destroyed. Jesus brings us out of the violence of this world through the gift of eternity, and sometimes in the very real midst of it.

Job 6:23 – We are ransomed from people who are ruthless, from adversaries or those who antagonize us. Got anyone like that in your life? Any frenemies out there? Yuck. It's good to know that Jesus doesn't just care about enemies, but that He cares about those people who use us as targets, who are fake friends, and offer sugary sweetness while "keeping us in our place."

Jeremiah 31:10-11 – We are ransomed from exile, from far off places, and strongholds. God brings us close to Him. He ransoms us from the people, places, and things that keep us from growing closer to Him, the roadblocks to belief, to faith, and to hope.

1 Peter 1:18-19 – We are ransomed from futile ways. Sometimes, we need saving from our own foolish selves. Sometimes we need saving from the generational sins that hold us captive and hold our families captive in destructive behaviors.

Sometimes we need saving from sins that keep the devil's thumb on us, holding us down, keeping us from growth.

He has brought us out. He has rescued us from whatever held us captive in the past and what we feel holds us captive now.
By any means necessary, He rescues us.

He treasures us. He brings us out. He would not leave one of us behind.

You are ransomed.

Exploration
Which of these verses did you need to hear most today and why?

What in your life has God brought you out of?

he calls me ransomed
▼ ▼ ▼

day two
The Rescue of Ransom

Have you ever just had a season? By season, I mean have you ever had a time of fighting the good fight, standing strong, and letting God hold up your arms when you thought you had nothing left?

Three years ago, our family found ourselves coming out of a season…finally. I could see the light at the end of the tunnel but was a little afraid to be overly hopeful. During one of those possibly-end-of-the-season days, we were driving from somewhere to something. Where or to what it was hardly matters. It was a regular day that I had stamped, "get through it" on. What I remember about this particular day was my husband and my nerves getting the best of me.

Our van radio was blaring a song and we have a general the-driver-controls-the-stereo rule.

"It's kind of loud, don't you think," I gently suggested to my driver-husband.

His response: Silence.

"No, I mean, it's really loud," I have a penchant toward impatience if you'd like to get a fuller picture here. I lean up to turn it down. Insert death glare from my husband, who is mostly low-key, mostly unopinionated, mostly lets me have my way.

I leaned back. Now, he's singing along.

What came out of my mouth next was not my best moment, "Dave, seriously, can't we turn it down? This is ridiculous. You're not even listening to me. It's TOO LOUD!"

My husband looked at me and his eyes turned a little sad, "Can't you hear it? Listen closer."

And so I did. I listened.

Dave had heard in the song the same message we hear when we read Isaiah 35:8-10. What particularly hopeful message do you find there?

What I didn't understand, but became crystal clear in a moment of really listening, was that I wasn't the only one who needed to know that God called me loved and that God called me ransomed, that God called me new. Dave needed to know too. Each of us need to know these truths. I had spent so much of my time concerned with my own needs, particularly in the struggle of the season, that I had failed to notice his. I responded to our season by raging against God, yelling at Him in the dark of night, and offering my tears as a living sacrifice of prayer.

My husband, however, was clinging to what He knew, what He had read in the Word, and been instructed in since he was a tow-headed toddler on chubby legs. This random song in that moment reminded him of the Biblical truths stored deep in His heart — he was God's. He was held by God. He was made new in Jesus Christ. God lifts our heads and God lifts our shame.

Isaiah 35 tells us we walk a road, even in trouble and difficulty, that is not shaming. We walk a road paved by the Savior of the world, who has gone before us. We will not be attacked by ravenous beasts, although sometimes it feels like it. We walk the road of the redeemed. The devil, he will try, but he may not have us. Jesus keeps us on the path, walking sure and strong, heads held high. Though we may feel like tucking our tails, hiding away beneath a rock, Christ is the one holding our faces high. His intercession for us reminds us to whom we belong…the Most High God. We are Holy, because He is Holy. We have been ransomed — brought out — of whatever has tried to overcome us.

In Christ, everlasting joy is on our heads — not guilt, not struggle, and certainly not shame.

Let's reflect on some other scriptural reminders of Who ransoms. According to Psalm 49:7-8, as well as Isaiah 49:15, why is Christ the only One who ransoms?

Jesus is King of Kings. Only He can save. Only He is enough. No person, no man, no ruler, no idea can rescue us, can bring us out and lift our heads as He can.

Only Jesus ransoms. He gave His life and He determines our value. He calls us worth ransoming.

Exploration
What other Scripture passages come to mind when you think of God paving the way, or God's work on a road/path?

What are some examples of things or seasons that trap people in shame and keep them from seeing their value in Christ Jesus?

What good have you seen God bring out of a difficult season, your own or someone else's?

he calls me ransomed
▼ ▼ ▼ ▼

day three
The High Price of Ransom

Let's play a word association game. I'll list a few words and next to each word you write anything associated with it that comes to mind. If nothing comes to mind, skim the first fourteen chapters of the Book of Exodus to jog your memory or to learn something new.

The Red Sea

Moses

The Passover Lamb

The Exodus

These are somewhat familiar stories for individuals who grew up in any church because we repeat them over and over again for children. In fact, God Himself wanted these stories in particular passed onto the next generation and the next, because He wanted His people to remember that He brought them out. What did He bring them out of in Exodus?

I'm not sure most of us can even imagine hard slavery like that, ever-increasing oppression, task masters, a life of clay with no straw, and drowned baby boys. Some of our ancestors risked life and limb to overcome slavery during the 19th century, and praise be to God for those who combat human trafficking and modern-day slavery. Slavery is one of the great injustices of humanity. God brings people out and today we find out just how ugly that work is, but God values freedom and He's not afraid of getting His hands dirty.

God references His work to free His people from Egypt's bonds in Isaiah 43:3-4. Read this passage and consider: What did God exchange for His people?

God is willing to give what is most valuable to Him in order to ransom His children.

This concept may be more than a little disturbing for us, God giving some people in exchange for others. To understand it better, we need to open our Bibles and return to Exodus, this time to the end. Near the end of the book, the Israelites cross the Red Sea into the land of promise, the land of freedom. Read Exodus 14:19-31. What was ransomed to save the people of Israel in this passage?

It should be hard to listen to the loss of the Egyptians. I don't think we were designed to be ok with people dying. We were made for life. Sin brought death into the world. We were made in the image of God, to have compassion and mercy for every life. We were also made to hold our heads high and that is impossible when we are sticking them in the sand. It's important to see the cost of ransom, just as much as the benefits of ransom. Matthew Henry reminds us in his commentary the reality of this ransom —

"God has purchased them dearly[iii]."

The salvation of the people of Israel, God's chosen ones, the people who were to bring the knowledge of Salvation to the rest of the world, was not a simple commercial transaction. Let us not assume that this was something easy or weightless to God. He gave dearly to ransom them from the hands of those who were destroying them.

When people lose their lives for any reason, God cares.

He cares for the murdered child, he cares for the aborted baby, he cares for the soldier. He cares.

I'm not entirely convinced that there weren't Egyptians turning to the Lord like mad under the weight of the closing waters of the Red Sea. They had seen His work, they had seen the miracles and plagues and the faithfulness of this unknown God. How many of them turned to Him, we do not know.

But in this instance, a ransom had to be given. It's hard. God came down as a pillar of fire, a cloud of darkness to stand between His people and the evil that would overtake them. He is not messing around when it comes to His children. Death is our earthly reality, yes, but don't be mistaken —

He is willing to let hard stuff happen if it means bringing us closer to Him.

That doesn't mean the hard stuff is a flashing neon sign of someone's lack of faith. That's silly and it's petty and it is not at all biblical. Faithfulness does not mean good will come to you, and unfaithfulness does not always bring on calamity. It does mean there are casualties in this war against the devil, sometimes it's us, sometimes it's our children, sometimes it's jobs or homes or happiness. And always, the battle is the Lord's. He is fighting.

Here is hope: He has won.

Revelation 5:9-10 tells us that Jesus came down, fought the fight, and won. The victory is ours for eternity:

> *And they sang a new song, saying,*
> *"Worthy are you to take the scroll*
>   *and to open its seals,*
> *for you were slain, and by your blood you ransomed people for God*
>   *from every tribe and language and people and nation,*
> *and you have made them a kingdom and priests to our God,*
>   *and they shall reign on the earth."*

Today we learn that ransoming comes with a price. This pilgrimage is hard. This journey is full of boundless love and joy, but also pain and struggle. Sometimes we need to get to the other side of the Sea to understand it. We can thank God for something He's doing that we don't quite understand. We can lay it at His feet, weep over those lost, and praise Him for eternal life in Jesus, offered free for every one of us, from those left standing and those drowned underwater.

He is working, ransoming, redeeming, and saving souls everywhere, every day. Rest in Him.

Exploration
Pray for anyone that God lays on your heart today, that His Salvation would be clearer today than it was yesterday for them, that He would reveal the ransom of His Son Jesus to them.

he calls me ransomed
▼ ▼ ▼ ▼

day four
All or Nothing Faith

Our youth Sunday School class decided to do something different this year. We wanted to open our Bibles, and to some extent our hearts, a little wider than might feel comfortable. It started out as fun and games. One day during Sunday School, we laid our Bibles on our laps and I had the youth holler out words that stuck out to them in Scripture, as they flipped through the pages. I asked them to look for big words, exciting words, sad words, confusing words, hard words, and encouraging words. Sometimes I think we take for granted the words of the Bible because they have become commonplace to us. As a believer of many years and an avid reader of Scripture, I'm constantly looking for Law and Gospel, guilt and grace, sin and salvation, but when I was young, I had no idea what to look for. If I'm honest, half the time, that's still true. I might read a passage about *ransom* but have no idea what the word itself means unless I take the time to sit, think, and explore.

Likewise, our study here is designed so that we glean something new from something we otherwise would have skipped over. Sometimes those things are desperately encouraging. Other times, I feel overwhelmed and perplexed by God's language and thoughts, and that's ok.

The Word was meant to be opened, whether comfortable or uncomfortable, understood or perplexing. God will always show us something. He is the Light. Would we rather remain in darkness?

Of course there's also the struggle of Pandora's Box. Sometimes that's what we get when we open the Bible — questions, questions, and more questions come pouring out.

Today's study deals with a very Pandora's Box topic. It's found in the Levitical law of the Old Testament and that's enough of a reason to be intimidated, uncomfortable. However, for all the reasons we just went over, we would be remiss if we skipped over it. I believe that God has something to reveal to us, even if only in part and confusing at face value. That said, let's dive in.

Please read Leviticus 27:28-29 in your Bible. Which things are to be kept from ransoming and why?

In the Old Testament God devoted some things to destruction. Some things were absolutely not meant to be redeemed. This conversation is related to concerns we probably have all had about the Old Testament, namely, that there is so much warfare! Goodness, they fought a lot back in the day. It is a culture from which we are so far removed, it may be hard to wrap our heads around. To begin to understand ransom and destruction and Israelite warfare, as well as its connection to us, we need to understand a Hebrew word we find in the Leviticus passage we just read through — *charam* or *cherem* — translated meaning *that which is to be given over to the Lord by destruction*[iv].

Note that *over to the Lord* is different than simple destruction. These four words — *over to the Lord* — help us to see purpose in all the destruction. Let that sink in and flash forward to your own life to grasp the concept further.

Sometimes we need a little *cherem* in our own lives. Sometimes there are jobs or material possessions or even relationships with others that should be utterly destroyed, that is to say removed from us, sent away, put on the trash heap- in order to honor the Lord. A scene from the movie Fireproof comes to mind. The main character struggled to overcome his pornography addiction. In the beginning of the movie, the main character dealt with it in a pretty cavalier manner. Then the day comes when his eyes were opened and he recognized that it was destroying everything he held dear. On that day, in the film, he carries his computer out into the driveway and smashes it to bits with a baseball bat. It was a perfectly good computer, but better off as *cherem* devoted to destruction before the Lord.

Can you identify anything else tied to a struggle that might be better devoted to destruction?

In the Old Testament, God's law said that things "devoted to destruction" were absolutely not to be ransomed. This was God's cut-and-dry command. But that computer just seems so darn useful. What reasons or excuses might people come up with not to destroy or set boundaries in situations you named above?

The Israelites also felt the same way and kept things back rather than giving them to the Lord, especially the sparkly and not-so-sparkly plunder from battles with other nations — cattle, currency, etc. Instead of heeding God's command, they often saved treasures, and sometimes people, that God did not intend to survive. You can see how it would be complicated. Just as in yesterday's study we talked about the sacrifice of the Egyptian army, likewise, the Israelites would go to battle with real people, people with families and homes.

However, the *cherem* was established in the Old Testament to keep the Israelites set apart. The people that came against them in war, or those God sent them against, were slowly destroying them. They introduced them to idols, led them to all manners of adultery, utterly destroying children and families, sometimes in days, sometimes months, or sometimes over years.

Here's the deal: **God values us enough to demand better.**

What can you see in your own life that God might want better for you?

The book of Isaiah can give us further answers and some peace. Turn to Isaiah 43:11-13 and note the relationship between God and the other things in our lives.

God gets to be God and we don't get to steal that from Him.

In the fullness of time, our God sent his own *cherem* — a Redeemer, a Ransom in Christ Jesus, our Lord.

Write this truth out by recording the words of Hebrews 10:10 in the space below:

We have been made holy through the sacrifice of the body of Jesus Christ once for all.

Jesus came and offered Himself for total destruction. It was confusing and hard for the disciples and the people who had to watch it. It invigorates and warms our hearts with grace, this sacrifice. But complacency, it does not create. God has set us apart with His ransom. Jesus has given His life for our salvation, and now we live in a New Covenant. We can offer grace and forgiveness at times when we could not see it without Him. There are definitely still times we need to send some stuff, that which leaves us complacent, to the trash heap – things and relationships that lead us away from Him — but we see it with a new mind…the mind of Christ.

With this new mind, we keep studying, opening the Word day after day to understand, especially when anything feels dark and confusing. This New Covenant calls us to go and Live. What encouragement does God give us in John 17:15-17?

We are different than the Israelites. We are called to go fully and unabashedly into the world and to do it with Bibles open, set apart but living out there in the world. We give Jesus our all, because He gave us every single bit of Himself.

All-in is the way we were made, but more importantly the way we were ransomed. We lift high that Ransom for all people. Share the message that destruction may last for a night, but resurrection comes in a sweet, sweet Savior.

Exploration
Pray for anyone touched by warfare today or anyone caught in addiction.

he calls me ransomed
▼ ▼ ▼ ▼

day five
The Ransom from Selfishness

Selfishness, never fun to talk about, but really an issue in all of our lives.

I so badly want to excuse it out of my life. I have a pretty decent list of reasons why it's not selfish, when I fill-in-the-blank…
 …rant at my family
 …pocket all my paycheck without sharing with those in need
 …eat all the chocolate in the chocolate cabinet before my family finds it
 …brush off a friend who could use a listening ear.

The list goes on and on. I'm a legitimately selfish person. I like my time spent on what I want to spend it on. I like my house to look the way I like it. I like my food to be what I want, when I want it. Since many of you don't know me, you may be thinking, "Wow. She might just need to get that problem under control." And I do. But so do you. ;)

Isaiah 47 tells all of us, each and every one of us, that we need to get this problem under control. Let's read a little of the Law, but don't worry, we'll get to the beautiful Gospel. Please open your Bible and read all of Isaiah 47. What words or phrases point to the selfishness God found in the Babylonians at that time?

Babylon was so much like those of us living in any first-world culture today. They thought they were all-that and a bag of chips. (FYI-my fourteen year old had to ask me what I meant by that phrase. It's a 1990's euphemism for thinking you're pretty great.) They had everything they needed – jobs, homes, good food, medical care, relative safety, and good coffee. Ok, maybe they didn't have good coffee, but you get the point. They felt secure in their pleasures and all the gifts that God had given them. The problem wasn't the gifts. It was where their trust lay.

The Babylonians had security in a few things that seriously hindered their ability to have a relationship with the Living God. My suggestion is that it would behoove us to take a peek at their issues, so maybe we can avoid or recover from a few of our own. We have a God who heals, who saves, so looking at our sin is never a problem, because we already live in the forgiveness He offers. Looking deeper allows us to really live in that forgiveness more authentically every day.

Let's go over six things the Babylonians put their trust in according to Isaiah 47.

Pleasure
If it felt good, if they felt good, and life was going well for them individually, than they were good to go. Who needs God when there's entertainment? What pleasures do we place our security in today?

A life without struggle, i.e. "The Good Life"
It's easy to feel secure when life is going well. Sometimes we look around us and we see others suffer and, sadly, we feel pretty darn secure because we're doing quite well, thank you. That won't ever happen to us. We must be really special people. Oh! It must be because we are such good people! (Note my sarcasm.) You can see how this train derails quickly. When we place our security in life going well for us, we have no solid foundation. What happens when we *do* experience loss? Where do we turn? How have you seen this in your own life or in the world around you?

Sorcery, talismans, astrology
We have one God. Searching after the stars, palm readers, horoscopes, lucky charms, psychics, and any other method to tell us our future or give us good stuff is expressively forbidden in the Bible. How do these things lead us away from trusting in the Lord our God?

Visible and invisible sin

Well, that hits the nail on the head. The Bible tells us that even when we think we are hiding it well from others, God sees our secret places. This may sound intimidating, but remember that the God who sees, also is the God who forgives. What have we to gain by confessing our sins and revealing the depths of our heart to God? Everything. Light, hope, mercy, grace, and peace, to name a few. How have you seen confession make a difference in being able to truly Live?

Wisdom and knowledge

What we *know* will never save us. What we believe saves us. If we put our trust in wisdom and knowledge to save us, we might miss Jesus Himself. When we are so busy searching science and religion for truth apart from His Word, we end up trusting human words and human ideas over God's. Scripture is meant to work in our hearts, as well as our minds. Faith is not something we can see from the outside. Only God knows someone's inner struggle. How have you seen wisdom and knowledge get in the way of faith? How have you seen them be a positive impact to faith?

Ourselves

The Babylonians thought they were so cool. Write the words of the last line of Isaiah 47:10 below:

Often times we think we're so cool too. What do we do, say, or think which reveals the parts of us that place our trust in ourselves and not in Christ?

Sometimes we can get so wrapped up in what we have, what we need, what we have going for us, that we forget from where it came, or from Whom it came. The reality is that it could all be gone in a flash, in the blink of an eye. And that would be ok. Because God would still be Savior of the world.

Tuck this proclamation into your heart —

"You are, and there is no one beside you, Jesus."

He is so good. God makes it so simple to turn to Him, to lay it down and rest in grace. He does all the work. We were dead in our trespasses, but as baptized children of God we are risen in new life! He raises us up from all that lack of trust and selfishness and grief, and puts on new clothes, white clothes, of Jesus' kindness, righteousness, and holiness.

"You are, and there is no one beside You, Jesus."

He *was* for the people of the Old Testament. He *is* for us today, and He *will be* tomorrow.

"You are, and there is no one beside You, Jesus."

Exploration

Of the six things in which the Babylonians trusted (see Isaiah 47 for a refresher), which do you see as the biggest issues in our world today?

Write a statement below, affirming God's place as the One worthy of putting your trust in. You can use my statement if you'd like - "You are, and there is no one beside You, Jesus." - or create your own.

he calls me child

Isaiah 43:4a
Because you are precious in my eyes,
and honored, and I love you…

week three
He Calls Me Child

Dr. Mom, Mortality, and Simply Being a Child
The Value of Children
Sons and Daughters
Planners and Pencils - I am His Child
Arise and Shine, Children

heart verse

Lift up your eyes all around, and see;
  they all gather together, they come to you;
your sons shall come from afar,
  and your daughters shall be carried
on the hip.
        Isaiah 60:4

he calls me child
▼ ▼ ▼

day one

Dr. Mom, Mortality, and Simply Being a Child

When we had our first baby, I was like, "I can handle this little ol' thing."

Breastfeeding was easy for me (THANK YOU, LORD!). Diaper changes and sleeplessness nights were hard, but seemed manageable with copious amounts of coffee. Granted, at this point there was only one of them and two of us, but you get the idea.

Then it happened — she got sick. And babies don't get normal-sick. They get weird-sick. There was all this snot that wouldn't come out. She couldn't breathe when I fed her. Her little chest found it challenging to rise and fall. I took her to the doctor, found out these symptoms evidently stemmed from an ear infection (WHAT?!!) and filled about fourteen prescriptions at the pharmacy, or maybe it was two prescriptions that felt like fourteen.

I hit a breaking point one day, picked up my phone, and called my pastor's wife, Linda. Crying as soon as she picked up, I lamented, "I don't think I can do this. I'm not cut out for parenting. I might need to turn her back in."

She got in her car, came to visit me, hugged all my tears out of me, and gave me comfort in the form of this phrase:

"I hate the Dr. Mom part of parenting too. Don't worry — It's God's job to keep them alive. It's your job to just love them."

Relief rushed over me. For weeks I had felt just so *responsible*. A tiny human dependent completely on me for survival was more than daunting, it seemed impossible. Of course it seemed impossible, because it was impossible...for me. It's God's job to keep them alive.

What part of illness do you most dislike or what part of being a mom is the hardest for you, whether it's emotional, practical, or plain gross?

In Isaiah 38 we find a section of narrative that offers a break from the poetic style common throughout Isaiah, for a story. An account, really, a true and real adventure in which King Hezekiah finds out very quickly that life is in God's hands and not His own. It's a useful lesson for all of us. Each of our lives are held tightly in the hands of God and God alone.

Open your Bible and read Isaiah 38:1-22. What struggle befell Hezekiah?

Fill in the missing words from Hezekiah's prayer in Isaiah 38:19.

The living, the living, he thanks you,
*   as I do this day;*
the ___father___ makes known to the
*   ___children___ your faithfulness.*

Hezekiah's prayer to our Father in heaven is so very real. So often we go about our lives in relative security and then in comes the hard stuff. When we face death, our eyes turn to the lasting, the spiritual. Almost any human being in those last moments, looking death smack dab in the middle of the eye, prays at the very least. Sometimes it's as simple as:

"Why, God?"
"Have mercy."
"Save me."

We all have our opinions about the existence of God, until mortality shows up on our doorstep, as it did for Isaiah. Suddenly, we need God like we have never needed Him before.

Isaiah's prayer goes through phases- anguish and uncertainty, to the embrace of mercy, and onto absolute certainty. Isaiah 38:10-20 may be one location in the Bible where the stages of grief was laid out for us long before any psychological theory existed.
　"I am consigned…"
　"…like a weaver I have rolled up my life…"
　"…like a lion he breaks all my bones…"
　"I moan like a dove…"
　"My eyes are weary with looking upward."
　"The Lord will save me."

Can you hear the physical and emotional struggle? Can you hear the doubt? The wrestling? What benefit is there for Hezekiah and for us as the reader, in writing out or praying aloud our struggle before the Lord of Hosts?

Hezekiah knew he was invited.

Remember what he proclaims in Isaiah 38:19 again:

> *The living, the living, he thanks you,*
>   *as I do this day;*
> *the father makes known to the children*
>   *your faithfulness.*

This is part of God's make-up. He is our Father. We are His dear children. He is not just King, although He reigns on the highest throne. He is not just Lord, although He is certainly Master over our lives. He is Father to His much-loved children. Hezekiah *may* be proclaiming his own desire to pass on God's faithfulness to his children, but He is certainly proclaiming God's faithfulness to us.

Just as Hezekiah proclaims his own place before the Lord, so this is your place to claim.

You are a child of God.

In Isaiah's psalms, God reassures me and whispers hope in my ear. The father does indeed make known to the children God's faithfulness, to each one of us. We are each His precious child. This Scripture, as does all Scripture, points us to our greater healing in Christ Jesus. We can share the Good News of God's salvation as Isaiah does in verse 20, because God the Father has left it right here in His Word for all of us to see and hear and be a part of.

Hezekiah is desperate to worship the Lord in response to His faithfulness (v.23), but the worship began long before recovery. The worship began with the eyes of a child raised up to the Father that longed to embrace him and tend to every wound. Before Hezekiah was at peace with what God was working in His life, he turned his face to Him in prayer. Those beginning stages of grief, given in prayer to God the Father, those are worship too.

Turn to Psalm 121:1-2 and read. What invitation to worship and prayer do you hear in these verses?

Raise your arms up today and let God hold you. In my opinion, the best part of the promise for Hezekiah is found early in the chapter. Look again at the first part of Isaiah 38:5 below:

> *"Thus says the LORD, the God of David your father: I have heard your prayer; I have seen your tears..."*

The strong arms of our Father sent Jesus Christ, His Son, to dry our tears with His death and resurrection. According to Revelation 21:4, one day those tears will be no more in heaven. This promise is for you and for your children, for you and every child of God around you.

Exploration

Glance through Hezekiah's prayer in Isaiah 38 again. What promise or truth, whether comforting or hard, sticks out to you?

Peek ahead to Isaiah 40:1. How does this verse speak of God's Fatherly affection for us?

he calls me child
▼ ▼ ▼ ▼

day two
The Value of Children

My little Zeke is adorable. When he was about 18 months he went through the developmental stage of find-Mom's-Bible-and-do-weird-stuff-to-it. You cannot fault the kid for thinking that the Word of the Lord is interesting. He ripped up most of Psalm 139 into itty bitty, almost unsalvageable pieces. There is a large hole in Psalm 139:22 through the end that I still have yet to find. He highlighted all of Matthew 19 and some of Matthew 20. He was evidently not bent on destruction, just discovery. I value my children growing up with Bibles sitting around, so I invested in my first Bible cover, which remains faithful to this day.

Children are special, no doubt. In Isaiah, we learn a little more of the value God places on children and why we are called to value them. Even if you translate this passage in the broader sense of children as all of God's people of any age, you can see why the application to the tiniest child of God is not missing.

Please read Isaiah 29:22-24. This is the Gospel at the end of a passage reminding Israel that unfaithfulness hurts. What gospel message do you hear when you read these verses?

What turns the tide of shame for the Israelites in this particular passage?

Ah, the promise of God working through children. Through this promise, God tells us He has a long-term plan.

Children give us hope. Their very presence in this world is a message of endurance from an unchanging God. The next generation reminds us that life will continue, despite the heartache and pain; a fresh new day, a new birth, will dawn.

Let's explore some things we can learn as God's children when we look at actual little children in the church and all around us.

Children bring honor to God.
> We praise God for the next generation, we recognize the miracle of life He has created, and we desire some kind of stability and morality for them. It spurs us on to consider and continue in the Faith. They help us to recognize that there is more than the moment before us, as we reflect on a longer-range plan which includes the next generation.

Children make us talk about God.
> In wanting to bring our children, or the children of the world, to a loving God, we talk about the Faith, we grow ourselves,

we open our hearts in ways we may not have otherwise. If we don't bring the topic of faith up, they have questions of their own, and it never dawned on them to keep their mouths closed, particularly concerning "politically incorrect" topics. Let us help them to feel comfortable enough to keep asking those questions. Let's spur on the next generation by talking about God and eternity.

Children are a mirror of our rebellion.
As much as I struggle with each of my children's rebellious spirits, I acutely feel the need for them to understand the reality of grace and forgiveness in their lives. When I look at my children, I see my own painful rebellion. I go my own way. I have my own ideas, although my Father in Heaven clearly knows best. Thank goodness for the family of God for me to fall on when I need mercy. Thank goodness that I can offer that living mercy to my children, even when we both have to endure the consequences for our painful actions.

Children mirror trust and faith.
Children get it sometimes when we don't. They can smell inauthenticity a mile away, but they also are willing to be all-in despite our weaknesses and flaws. They lean on God in simple prayers and don't need all the bells and whistles to bring them to meet with the Savior; a conversation, a small craft to hang in their room, simple relationship is enough to keep them coming back to church and learning about God again and again.

Read Isaiah 29:24 again. Write it out in the space below:

This small verse holds a promise for when we travel our own ways, and when our children travel their own paths, away from God. He knows the prodigal. He sees their struggle. He hears the grumbles and the moans, the ranting, and the hiding. He brings us back to Him. The lost are found in Him, according to Luke 15.

Malachi 2:10 reminds us that we should extend grace based on this title – Child of God:

> *Have we not all one Father? Has not one God created us? Why then are we faithless to one another, profaning the covenant of our fathers?*

Abortion is not ok. Pouring judgment out on our unbelieving neighbor is also not ok. Leaving them without the Gospel of Jesus, also not ok. Placing less value on the high schooler's opinion in church than the middle-aged leader is not ok. Leaving the elderly in loneliness is not ok. We are all sinners, but by the name of Jesus we are saved and by His grace alone.

Today, look at a child. Let them know that they are seen. Let them know that their very presence glorifies the name of the Living God, our Creator. Embrace that childlike-faith part of yourself. Sing a round of Jesus loves me, pray before bedtime, and thank the Lord for being faithful to each and every generation.

Exploration

What do you remember about your faith walk as a child? What or who spoke God's love over you as you were growing?

What children do you interact with on a regular basis? How do you share faith in Jesus with them?

Find one way to share God's Word and Grace with someone under the age of 18 this week. Share your idea in the space here, or with your group!

he calls me child
▼ ▼ ▼

day three
Sons and Daughters

The Book of Isaiah itself is such a gem. My study Bible tells me that no other book is quoted more frequently in the New Testament as Isaiah, and some commentators refer to it as the Fifth Gospel[v]. In just three weeks of our eight-week study, I think you can see why. Isaiah holds so much promise, without ignoring our sinful state. It recognizes our need and His willingness to be our Savior.

Today we return to Isaiah 43. It's fair to say that I am in love with this chapter of Scripture. It brings us both God's Law and God's Gospel in harmony. We can see our own rebellion in it, as well as the promise of a Savior. It is also beautifully written and screaming to be shared with someone.

Open to Isaiah 43 and see how God speaks to all nations through His prophets. Read Isaiah 43:4-9. Who is God bringing together according to this passage?

God communicates His love for people from every nation here. This reminder comes immediately after God declares,

> *"I give men in return for you, peoples in exchange for your life…"* (Isaiah 43:4)

God is nothing if not congruent. When the world would claim that the Bible contradicts itself, verses like this help us to see the fullness of God. Our own understanding comes when He opens our eyes to the page. What exhortation is at the very beginning of Isaiah 43:5 as a pivot in the passage?

We may not understand completely what God is doing at any given time, or ever! But He promises His presence.

> *"Fear not, for I am with you…"* (Isaiah 43:5)

In these verses He says in effect,

> *I know this is hard to understand. I know there is sacrifice. I know that it's confusing.*
> *But fear not! I am still here. I am still God over all.*
> *I do care. I am Love.*
> *I'm giving each and every human being on this Earth the opportunity to be my child.* (author's paraphrase)

How does God refer to those he is gathering from the ends of the earth? What titles does He give them in Isaiah 43:6?

I like the mental picture of being God's child. I love the picture of resting safe in His strong arms, looking to Him as a faithful and true parent, with concern and grace and wisdom to share.

But even more...I want to be His daughter.

My dad died when I was about 18-months-old. Until recently, I hadn't realized what an impact his death had on my life. Every girl needs a dad. Someone to tell her she's pretty, someone that lights up when she walks into the room, and someone to teach her that her value isn't held by man, but by God. If you haven't had this in your life, I'm very sorry. Often, but not always, God fills in the gaps with other people in our lives. Sometimes we have only Him. If this was or is your reality, I know it's hard. It is a huge loss. Mourn it. Give it to Him. Perhaps you are the one that can understand, better than any of us, the need we each have for our Faithful Father God. If you are willing, share your own experiences and relationship you have had with a father or father-figure.

My step-dad adopted me when I was 5 years old. He never fails to make me feel like the prettiest girl in the room. He gets up at 6am to make me breakfast sandwiches and good coffee when I visit, not wanting to miss even a moment of conversation together. He stands in the driveway when I pull my minivan out to head back to Ohio. When I round the bend...sometimes he's still standing there.

God is our father twice over. He made and created us. For proof of this, look back at Isaiah 43:7. Then, he adopts us through the sacrifice of Jesus Christ and the gift of faith by His grace. We'll go deeper into this adoption process tomorrow. For today, let's find foundation for claiming ourselves to be His daughters.

Please turn to Mark 5:21-43, or you can go rogue with the parallel passages in Luke 8 and Matthew 9. However, keep in mind that Mark is the most complete account. Highlight, underline, or note each time the words *daughter*, *child*, or *little girl* are utilized in the reading.

When Jesus sees us, he doesn't just see a mass of people. He is concerned with the communal, the group, the body of believers, the nations…but He is also concerned with our inherent uniqueness. It strikes me that Jesus asks the question, "Who touched Me?" (Mark 5:31), not for His own benefit, but for hers. The woman was already healed immediately when she touched His robe.

Jesus reaches out and invites her into relationship with one word – daughter.

What name does Jesus call Jairus's daughter in Mark 5:41?

Talitha is an Aramaic word. It is a very unique phrase, a feminine word, specific to young women. Strong's Concordance asserts that it is more correctly translated maiden or even damsel[vi]. Jesus is no fairy tale, but He knows a girl's heart, for sure.

Daughter, maiden, little girl, child, beloved. Could we want for more endearment? Which one of these titles given to you by God speaks to you the most and why?

Jesus fills in all the gaps where life has left us empty. We have a perfect God who declares us Sons and Daughters of the One True King. He is so faithful.

Exploration

How do you think the relationship with our earthly father is a blessing and how can it be confusing for our relationship with God?

What terms of endearment mean the most to you, in Scripture, in your marriage, in your family, anywhere?

What loving words and names speak grace and love into your life?

he calls me child
▼▲ ▼▲ ▼▲ ▼▲

day four
Planners and Pencils: I am His Child

I am a list maker.

I love to-do lists and plotting and planning. I still use a paper planner. I tried the iPhone version and it just never took. I like to see things laid out in ink, nice and clear, well, pencil. I only write in my planner in pencil because guess what...plans change, right? As much as I'd like my plans to work out the first time, I would say that 75% of the time, I find myself applying eraser to my planner and trying out plan B, sometimes plan C, sometimes plan D, E, F, G, or Z.

Isaiah has something to say about planning also. Open your Bible and read Isaiah 30:1-11. What appears eye-opening in this passage? What sins does God outline for His people here?

The mirror of sin is strong with this one. Two segments really stick out to me, in connecting the pieces of sin and our study of the word *child*.

Read Isaiah 30:1 again below. Circle the adjective, or descriptor, related to us as God's children in this verse:
> "Ah, stubborn children," declares the Lord,
> "who carry out a plan, but not mine,
> and who make an alliance, but not of my Spirit,
>   that they may add sin to sin;

How often do I carry out, or more accurately, attempt to carry out plans of my own, rather than the Lord's? I'm actually in a situation right now, as I type, that makes me want to go one direction, when I know the Lord is calling me to wait on His direction.

Have you ever been in a situation where you avoid hearing God's Truth because you have a better idea? If you have, please share!

I don't think it's just me. God's Word in Isaiah really points out the path of original sin we all find ourselves walking. The Old Adam in us wants to plan and plot and follow our own way. In Christ, and only in Christ, can we tell Old Adam to talk to the hand. In our baptisms, Christ Jesus raises us as believers that can do a new thing. We can turn in a new direction.

We are no longer *children unwilling to hear* as it says in Isaiah 30:9.

We are sons.

Look up the following verses and share what joy of sonship you learn about in each.

    John 1:12-13

    Ephesians 1:3-6

    Galatians 4:4-5

We are adopted into a better plan.

Bring on Your plans, Lord. Erase mine all you want. I give it to you.

Exploration

Are you a planner person? How important is planning to you?

What area of your life could you use more flexibility?

Write a prayer that acknowledges God as the keeper of the schedule and ask for His help with all of life's plan you are faced with in this season of your life.

he calls me child
▼ ▼ ▼

day five
Arise and Shine, Children

Today we will be reading some words that may be very familiar for some of you. Let's see if we can open the Word and hear it afresh. Turn to Hebrews 4:12 in your Bible and write that verse in the space below:

For the word of God is living + active.

The Word is surely living. Never doubt that. The Bible is different than any other book. It works with the Spirit in our hearts, in our minds, in our lungs, and our legs. When we take it up, it breathes fresh life into our veins and strengthens us for the day ahead, or calms our souls for a night of rest.

Please read the living words of Isaiah 60:1-4 in your Bible and write the first two words of the passage nice and large:

ARISE; SHINE

While this verse talks about the light of Christ dawning in our life as belief and faith, don't miss the significance of the term *arise*. The two are connected.

Isaiah 60:1-4 proclaims a prophecy of the Messiah yet to come, Jesus Christ, Word made flesh. When He came to earth, to take the weight of our sin and punishment upon the cross, darkness prevailed for a moment, but light dawned eternal. Read each of the following verses and note what famous account is witnessed through each.

>Luke 24:1

>Mark 16:9

>John 20:1

What detail does John add that the other Gospel writers were not called to add?

There are days in our lives when it is still dark.

This was the reality for the Israelites. The world, the sin taking over their lives and the world around them was darkness. Darkness like this is accompanied by a loss of hope. They became a people sitting on the ground aching for problems they could not solve for themselves or in themselves. What things in the world around you have you aching for all the problems, feeling the weight of hopelessness?

Arise, shine, for your light has come...

Isaiah 60:1 prophesies something more for us. This prophecy of Jesus is complete for us living in the days after Christ's death and resurrection. When we lose hope for the world in which our children will have to grow up, when we wonder if the next generation will be able to hold strong, if *we'll* be able to hold strong, there is hope - *The Light* has come. The Light itself has arisen. It has walked from the tomb, while it was still dark, and the darkness will NOT overcome it.

Our children, the next generation walking this earth, are His children. The promises held in Isaiah 60:4 are as true for us, as they were for the nation of Israel. He will not forsake us. We are not a people of death and destruction. We are a people of Life and Eternity.

What promise do you hear in Proverbs 14:26-27?

What title do you find for yourself in John 12:36?

We are believers. The radiance of the Son lives in us (Isaiah 60:5). Let the world see it. You are a treasure to Him. Your children, and your children's children, are a treasure to Him. The people God puts in your path are a treasure to Him.

Arise. Let Him Radiate. Let the Sonlight reflect off your face and your hands and your feet as you receive His forgiveness and life-giving Word.

Your Light has come.

Exploration

Are you a morning person? What part of the day do you like best? Least?

What promise of the Resurrection do you hold most dear? How have you seen it work in your life in the last few weeks or months?

Alright, time for some Gospel-motivated action. Choose one specific way you can shine the Light of the Resurrection to a person or in a place, somewhere, anywhere, this week, using either your face, your hands, or your feet.

he calls me redeemed

Isaiah 43:4a
Because you are precious in my eyes,
and honored, and I love you…

week four
He Calls Me Redeemed

Creation, Evolution, and Redemption
Name-calling and the Gospel
Written in Iron Ink
Not Forgotten
Someone Find Me a Kinsmen-Redeemer

heart verse
Can a woman forget her nursing child,
that she should have no compassion
on the son of her womb?
Even these may forget,
yet I will not forget you.
Isaiah 49:15

he calls me redeemed
▼ ▼ ▼ ▼

day one
Creation, Evolution, and Redemption

Every time I make dinner for my family, I feel a little attached to it – the food, not the family. I drag all the ingredients out of the fridge, slightly begrudgingly. I clang around the pots and pans, setting them out on the stove. I lay veggies out on the counter. I start to chop and dice. I begin to see the colors and think on what spices I want to add. I hear the sizzle of oil as it starts to clarify in my bright red Dutch oven. I mix and I stir and I ponder and I create. I begin to get excited. I set out our eclectic collection of cloth napkins. I hustle and I invite to the table. We all sit down and then everyone starts talking…

"Ugh, what's this green stuff?"

"Why did you put onions in here?"

"Well, I'll eat this part, but there is no way I'm eating that."

But...but...but...I want to say, "I *made* that!!! I *worked hard* on that. That is my *creation*!"

Now, consider this scenario side by side with our responses so often to the Maker of the Universe. He is maybe less of a giant baby about it, but He looks on us as more than a hastily thrown together sandwich. We are the well-planned, carefully crafted family dinner. He made us with His own hands. He breathed His own breath of life into each of us.

Open your Bible to Genesis 2:5-7 and identify anything that points to the care and crafting of our Heavenly Father.

God is a creator, the Creator. We are His thoughtful creation.

This is an important concept as we learn about His title, Redeemer. Read Isaiah 44:21-24 and again list anything in the verses that signifies God's thoughtfulness regarding His creation.

Today we'll work through each verse in slow motion together.

> *Return to Me, for I have redeemed you.*

The first time we hear *redeemed* in the passage is in Isaiah 44:22. God points back to the very beginning, to creation. *Return to Me* recognizes that we were in relationship with God from the beginning, whether we recognize it or not. The preceding verse, Isaiah 44:21 clarifies that relationship -

I formed you...you will not be forgotten by me.

God redeems us because He is our Father and our Maker.

The concept of evolution not only picks away at our value as the children of God, but it messes with the concept of our *redemption* by God as well. Let's see if we can see the creation and redemption connection in a fresh light.

The same Hebrew root word is used in every reference to redemption in Isaiah 44:22-24 – *gaal*[vii]. There are two Hebrew roots for redemption found throughout the Old Testament, *gaal* and *padah*. They both mean essentially the same thing – redeem, ransom, rescue, redemption price, buy back, etc. However, *gaal* has one major difference. It insinuates close relationship.

Gaal has a strong connection to the Old Testament concept of *kinsman-redeemer*, which we will study later this week. What you need to know for now is that it is a relational word. It is redemption by a close relative, a kinsman, or a family member of some sort.

Redemption in Isaiah 44 has to do with being redeemed by God our Father, by Jesus our brother – not a stranger. God wants to buy us back because He formed us and crafted every part of us, and He redeemed us to adopt us into His family.

What helpful reminders of this do you find in Ephesians 2:4 as well as a few verses later in Ephesians 2:10?

You are redeemed because you were loved from the beginning. You are a work of art. God crafted your being, your DNA, your atoms and substance, your hair, your nails, your fingerprints. He birthed you and brought you into the light of day (Isaiah 44:24)…of course He's going to redeem you!

Isaiah 44:23 tells us there is more to the story…

The whole earth sings Redemption songs

This verse is so full of joy that it bursts from the page:
> Sing, O heavens, for the LORD has done it;
>   shout, O depths of the earth;
> break forth into singing, O mountains,
>   O forest, and every tree in it!
> For the LORD has redeemed Jacob,
>   and will be glorified in Israel.

Why are the mountains, the forests, and every single tree singing?

He created all of it. He wove each piece of this earth, fashioned each tall oak and every stout little flower. They are part of the redemption song. They sing Jesus's praise every day. If you read Isaiah 44 carefully, it's not because of their own restoration, which is to come in fullness when Jesus returns and ushers in the New Creation. No, it is because Israel, God's people, have been redeemed. Wow!

Birds tweet a song –
> "You are redeemed."

Mountains stand tall with joy –
> "You are redeemed."

Trees sway and leaves rustle –
> "You are redeemed."

He does not leave us, nor forsake us; we will not be forgotten. We are His, in both creation and in redemption.

Exploration

What have you learned in the span of your life that helps you to stand strong in God as Creator? These might be Bible verses, a teacher's influence, an experience, etc.

What is one of your favorite parts of His creation, beyond people, i.e. the rest of the natural world?

he calls me redeemed
▼ ▼ ▼ ▼

day two
Name-calling and the Gospel

There's a fun place in Isaiah 41, where God uses a little name calling to get our attention. This verse sticks out as an oddity, so it begs to be studied. At first glance, it doesn't seem like a verse you would share to reach someone with the love of Jesus. Many might consider it more than a hint offensive, but the redemption promise in it is so clear. I hope you are itching to share it by the end of today's study.

Please read Isaiah 41:14-15. What derogatory terms or descriptions can you identify?

I don't know about you, but I prefer not to think of myself as a worm. In fact, this is crazy counter-cultural. Most of us, in our current cultural context, like to think that we are pretty good people, or at the very least, decent people. We are average-citizen-kind-of people, aren't we?

God's honesty in this circumstance is our salvation.

Jacob was a worm. We are a worm.

It is what it is. We stink it up. We put ourselves before other people. We hold our earthly treasures tight to our hearts. We disregard God on some level, daily. We consider ourselves in such a way that we push His Spirit further down, so we don't have to listen to the Truth that shakes us to our core – we need Him. Without Him, we are dust, worms along the ground. We are here one day, and then dried up in the sunshine the next.

Paul, the apostle, missionary of the Early Church, dynamic speaker, teacher, and child of God, has something to say on the matter as well. Investigate the verses below and identify any insight about the state of our goodness you might find.

1 Timothy 1:15-16

Romans 7:21,24-25

Where does Paul claim any of our goodness comes from?

Now, read Isaiah 41:14 again below and circle the answer to this goodness problem of ours:

> *Fear not, you worm Jacob,*
>   *you men of Israel!*
> *I am the one who helps you, declares the LORD;*
>   *your Redeemer is the Holy One of Israel.*

Redemption is the answer. Help is the answer.

God gives us the Law. He doesn't mess around with prettying it up. We are sinful. We need a Savior. Then, He goes beyond that and gives us more. He gives us something better.

We have a Helper.

Christ, as our Redeemer, and through the Holy Spirit in us, is also the Help we need. What sweet Gospel Truth! I don't know about you, but most days I need some *help*. I don't need Him to pretty it up. I need real and constant help — for myself, for my children, for my church, and for my life.

Part of the Gospel of redemption is that He is here to *help*. Let's let Him. Let's turn to His Word and turn to prayer. Our salvation is 100% secure in Jesus Christ, we have nothing to add, or to fear. We can let Him root around a little in us and in our lives, allowing Him full access to our hidden parts, which He sees anyway, to do His good work in complete assurance of His goodness and mercy.

Isaiah 41:15 tells us that when it's the worm against the mountain of life, the worm in Christ wins.

Read Psalm 124:8 and write it in some seriously large handwriting below.

Say it loud and strong.
Call on His name with me.

My help is in the name of the Lord!
Father, we come to You. We give You thanks for Your Word and Your Truth. You have redeemed us. You have rescued us from the low place. You raise us up with Your Son. We trust in You. We honor You. We ask You to continue this work in our lives today and every day. Spirit, change our hearts, change our minds, change our lives as You draw us closer to the Father every day. Thank you for seeing us, Lord. Thank you for being faithful when we are not. Fill us with Your Grace, now and always. You are everything, Lord. Everything. In Jesus' name we pray. Amen.

Exploration

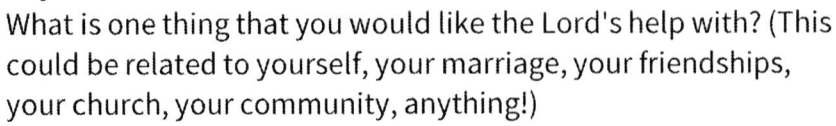

What is one thing that you would like the Lord's help with? (This could be related to yourself, your marriage, your friendships, your church, your community, anything!)

He is already there, but let's bring it before Him. Take a moment to pray for His help with this specific thing today.

Write Psalm 124:8 on a sticky note or notecard, anywhere, today. Take a picture and share it with your friends on social media. Share it wherever, with whomever. Rejoice! You are the face of Christ's mercy to someone who needs to hear and see it today (v.16).

he calls me redeemed
▼ ▼ ▼ ▼

day three
Written in Iron Ink

What are some of your favorite ways in which God comes to you?

Many Christian denominations specifically teach three particular ways, or means, in which God comes to us. These three ways are through His Word (the Bible), in our baptisms, and in the Lord's Supper. Your belief system might be a touch different, but I doubt that it strays much from these three connectors. We need God like fish need water, and more than that. Our deepest need in this life is for God. We will scramble any which way until our hearts settle in His arms. Thankfully, God, does not remain hidden. He has left these three — the Bible, Baptism, and the Lord's Supper — that are both physical and spiritual — to come to us. God loves worship. He loves praise and He loves His created things, water, bread, and wine, but our worship is intended to connect these to His Son and these are intended to connection our hearts to His promises in His Word. The beauty is that when we understand that He comes in these three sure and certain ways, each attested to in His Word, then we are no longer searching and searching. Instead, we know we have been *found* by Him.

If all of that last paragraph sounded like theological mumbo jumbo to you, rest in this:

God comes.

God comes to you.
Let's return to Isaiah 43 once again and study this concept. Start by reading Isaiah 43:1 below. If you feel so led, write this verse out in a notebook, on scrap paper, on your shoe, wherever, to commit it deep into your heart. Who is taking action in this passage?

Note: God is the seeker. He calls and we answer. Before you were born, He called you. Before your parents, your grandparents, or you brought yourself to church, He called you. Before baptism, before confirmation, before growth…He called you.

God calls you by your name.
Heidi, David, Macee, Jonah, Jyeva, Ezekiel

This is my family. Each with their own name. He called each of us and He called each of us individually by our names. What is your name? Write it out in the space below. What are the names of those closest to you? Include their names as well.

By calling you, God brings you into His redemptive plan, by this name. He writes the name of each believer in His Book of Life (Rev. 20:12) and on His heart.

Then, He keeps writing.
The book of Job shares a unique way that God reveals Himself to those around us, still in connection with His Word. Please read Job 19:23-24 and look for God's promises in the middle of Job's struggle.

Job's life was not so easy. The first part and the last part of it was pretty good. The middle was all kinds of gunky and hard. Loss, ongoing health problems, cruddy friends, embarrassment, marriage issues. The list goes on and on for our friend Job. His physical, earthly problems bubbled up into a spiritual crisis. In the verses just read, Job attests to what he wanted from God in all the gunk.

Most of us would want the same thing in similar circumstances:

Job cries out to God,

"Make it count! Don't leave me here. Do something with this!"

"If I am going to go through all of this, I want it to matter."
(Heidi's personal paraphrases)

What Job wanted is what God does indeed give to each of us — a testimony of His work, written in Iron Ink. It is un-erasable. It is durable. This testimony is able to withstand the arguments and the questioning in our own soul. Through the testimony of His work in our lives, God gives us a legacy going out for generations to come — to our families, our churches, and our communities.

Read Job's somewhat famous testimony, written in the Iron Ink of Scripture in Job 19:25-26. Paraphrase this portion of Scripture for me in your own words. What is the gist of God's promises that Job proclaims for us to hear?

God comes to others through our testimony of Jesus Christ. He reaches into this world through each of us, so that others can begin to see the great Redeemer. They will know Him by who we are and where we have been, and the Word we share because of it.

Flip back to Isaiah 43. This time scroll down to verses 14 and 15. What prophecy of a messy life for the Israelites do you find there?

Babylon is not a happy prophecy for Israel. Israel is about to have a Job moment. Right after the proclamation of grace in Isaiah 43:1, "I have called you by name, you are mine," God brings hard news to His people. It's about to get messy. Babylon means bondage. Babylon means slavery. They will be sent far away, their national identity destroyed, families split up, livelihoods decimated. This is messy stuff. But God's message isn't just "messy is coming." His message for us in Job is —

I use the messy.

It is no mistake that God calls Himself Redeemer in this passage. You are Mine, He says, when life comes at you, when you walk through the fire, when bondage overtakes you, people will see My redemption story. Fill in the missing pieces of Isaiah 43:14 below:

Thus says the LORD,

    your Redeemer, the Holy One of Israel:

"For _____ _____ _____

    _____ to Babylon

and bring them all down as fugitives,

    even the Chaldeans, in the ships in which they rejoice.

All of this, so that He can redeem. So that they will know redemption.

We are iron ink. Every time we share His Word and His testimony in our lives, He comes.

He comes for you.

He comes for me.

He comes for them.

He comes – Redeemer, Holy One, Creator, King.

Watch Him write.

Exploration
What iron ink testimony has God written or is writing in your life?

How has He used this testimony to share His redemption with others?

What Bible verses or passages speak His life into your story?

he calls me redeemed
▼▼▼▼

day four
Not Forgotten

So much of childhood is wrapped up in our search for belonging. We want to belong in our families, from the oldest trying to please and excel, to the middle child vying for attention or trying not to fade into the wallpaper, and the youngest putting out sparks of humor and zest to liven up the party. These are sweeping generalizations but at least they're research-based generalizations, right? What commonalities have you found to be true based on birth order?

What birth order generalizations do you disagree with?

You or I may not "fit" the mold, but one thing our birth order tells us is that we all want to belong. We want to fit, even when we are trying ever so hard to be rogue. Developmentally, our parents approval often means the world to us growing up, even if they were MIA. Our siblings' opinions also mattered, whether they understood that or not. Our teachers and peers and youth leaders, we wanted them to see us. We may not have begged for attention, but we didn't want to be forgettable. Who wants to be forgotten.

We want to belong and to be remembered. It's why infants cry to alert us to needs, preschoolers ask for band-aids every 47 seconds, and teenagers try out new outfits and attitudes daily. Even as adults, we make drama where there's peace, we try to buy the very best and newest stuff, and we add friend after friend to our Facebook feed…the task of being unforgettable is exhausting.

Today we find out the Jesus-truth on this matter.

We are never forgotten. We are anything but forgettable.

Please open your Bible and read Isaiah 49:13-17. What images does God use in this passage connected to *not forgotten*?

He cannot forget. All this vying for attention in our lives is really a search for the One who cannot forget us, even if He tried. The questions God asks of Israel here are harder than they may appear at first glance, such as Isaiah 49:15:

> *"Can a woman forget her nursing child?"*

Some of us may say, "No, of course not!"

Others of us may say, "My mom did."

Can you see how life complicates our ability to see Truth? Maybe this knowledge can give us compassion for those who still wrestle and are disconnected from church or Faith.

God understands this complication. Listen again to the next Words from Isaiah 49:15 —

> *"Even these may forget, yet I will not forget you."*

God further drives home His promise with another visual in Isaiah 49:16 —

> *"Behold, I have engraved you on the palms of my hands..."*

God makes promises to the city of Jerusalem, but the residents of those walls heard the promise in it for their own lives. When siege laid waste and Babylon breaks through the city walls, terror and fear struck every heart and every family. Their city was destroyed, and the Temple, God's dwelling place among them, was also destroyed. Each of those people needed to hear this message, "I am not forgotten. My God is with me." God's plan was redemption.

To attest to this redemptive plan, He wrote the promise on His hands.

On His hands, He engraved our names. He engraved the name of His Church, His people.

He could not, would not forget.

Turn to Isaiah 63:7-16, in your Bible. What else does God remember, according to these verses? Where can you see God's plan of redemption in them, for the nation of Israel at that time, and for us today?

Even when others fail to acknowledge us, God in Trinity remembers us.

Glance at Isaiah 63:7-16 a second time and look for the work of each member of the Trinity in our Redemption. What evidence did you find?

Here are a few thoughts from my own vantage point of the text in order of Father, Son, and then Holy Spirit:

"You are our Father…" - Isaiah 63:16
　There's that familial language again. We need not look any further than to our Father in Heaven to acknowledge us, to recognize us, or to see us. As children or as adults, we are not forgotten.

"In all their affliction, he was afflicted, and the angel of his presence saved them…" - Isaiah 63:9
　The Angel of the Lord is believed by Old Testament scholars to speak of God's Son before His incarnation. This is Jesus, plain and simple. He was afflicted for us. He saves us. He loves us. He looks upon us and redeems us.

"Where is he who put in the midst of them his Holy Spirit..." - Isaiah 63:11

God places the Holy Spirit into our midst and into each of us. The Spirit's work is connected to remembrance. The Spirit isn't only for our remembrance of God, but His remembrance of us as well. God sees us through the work of His Spirit in Jesus Christ. He remembers us as faithful children, because of the Spirit's faithfulness in us. We might grieve the Holy Spirit by our rebellion (v. 10), but there is a promise there, beyond the threat of discipline. God sees our rebellion because *He sees us*. Only in having our rebellion, our sin laid bare, can redemption enter in. Thank you, Holy Spirit for seeing *all* of me – and loving me anyway! (See also Isaiah 63:10, 14.)

Aren't His promises remarkable? We are not forgotten. No matter what this life and this world may hold, our Redeemer of Old is bigger, greater, and more steadfast than anything we encounter in this life. We want to leave a lasting mark in this life, we want to be remembered, and in Christ, we know we are remembered in the only place that matters— on God's hand — engraved on His hands and held by His Spirit.

You are not forgotten.

Exploration
Sometimes I think we speak of the Trinity in vagueness, because it is a slightly vague and complex idea to us. Which person of the Trinity gives you comfort today and in what way —Father, Son, or Holy Spirit?

Who can you share the message of *not forgotten* with?

he calls me redeemed
▼▼▼▼

day five
Somebody Find Me a Kinsmen-Redeemer

Sometimes there are Biblical concepts that we could skip over. They wouldn't lessen our faith if we didn't know about them. They wouldn't change anything about our belief system, but they would *grow* our faith if we learned about them. Today, we're going to stretch ourselves and grow with this question —

What is a kinsmen-redeemer?

And...

Why do I care?

I know Old Testament scholars probably have their mouths hanging open from my lack of propriety. Well, if they read my stuff. More important to me though, is acknowledging when we get intimidated and embarrassed by our lack of Bible knowledge and it hinders us from turning the pages. Let's not get trumped up by that. The message of Scripture is always redemption. Be assured that every word points to a greater message of grace found in Jesus. So we study and we dig deeper.

Please hustle over to the book of Ruth and find out just what this kinsman-redeemer business is all about.

I think a brief synopsis may be useful here: Ruth is Naomi's daughter-in-law. Generally speaking, Ruth's faithfulness is met with great esteem in the Scriptures and in our churches. She leaves everything behind, including her own culture's gods, in love and solidarity for her mother-in-law. That alone is worth noting. She could have stayed in the familiar, the comfortable, but she followed Naomi into the uncertain, into poverty, and into the unknown. In doing so, Ruth embraced an unknown God. This is surely a work of the Holy Spirit writing Ruth's testimony for us on the page. However, without a husband, these two women were broke. Not America broke, but third-world-country broke. They had nothing. They could own nothing. They were at the mercy of family to literally lift them up from the dust — to redeem them.

Jewish Old Testament law afforded for a workable solution to this problem. What stipulations do you find for redemption, from poverty and destitution, within the family of God recorded in Leviticus 25:23-25, 47-48?

This is just a small snippet of the Old Testament law, but it gives us the background we need. Now let's jump into Ruth and Naomi's story a couple of chapters in to the Book of Ruth. Please read all of Ruth 2, paying special attention to Ruth 2:19-22. What characters do we find in the account at this point?

Ruth and Naomi were broke, remember. They gleaned from the fields for their food. Boaz's first kindness was to let Ruth walk behind the workers in his fields and pick up the fallen grain to eat. Boaz offered hope from starvation here. In Ruth 2:20, Naomi recognizes this is the Lord working through Boaz, showing His great faithfulness. Look at her quote again...

> "...the Lord, whose kindness has not forsaken the living or the dead!"

Not forsaken was something Naomi and Ruth needed to see. Hungry, grieving, alone – God gives us hope. The Lord is always holding us in His hands.

Boaz's second kindness is reported by Ruth herself, in Ruth 2:21. You can imagine the protection a young woman would need in the middle of a field alone. God works through Boaz, protecting Ruth. When have you seen God protect you through actual people in your own life, whether parents, siblings, family, friends, church family, or a stranger?

We find a third kindness from Boaz back in Ruth 2:20. He is Ruth's kinsman-redeemer. He has the duty, according to the law of Leviticus 25, to buy her life back from the forsakenness of widowhood, to lift her out of the dust. In the end you'll see that he also chooses to give her something more — honor.

This is how Christ comes to us. He is charged by the Father with the duty of redeeming the brothers and sisters. God made us. He calls us children, but sin separates us from Him. Jesus is sent as our Kinsmen-Redeemer, our Savior who breaks the power of sin in the disconnect of our relationship with God.

Jesus brings us back into the family.

Jesus gave up His honor, for a time, to bestow it upon us, humbling Himself to walk our fields, to glean for souls on this soil, because He is our brother, our Kinsman-Redeemer.

Look for Ruth and Naomi's own experience with redemption and the Lord's faithfulness in Ruth 4:13-17 below. Underline the words of praise to our Redeemer, through the lips of women to Naomi in the passage:

> *So Boaz took Ruth, and she became his wife. And he went in to her, and the L*ORD *gave her conception, and she bore a son. Then the women said to Naomi, "Blessed be the L*ORD*, who has not left you this day without a redeemer, and may his name be renowned in Israel! He shall be to you a restorer of life and a nourisher of your old age, for your daughter-in-law who loves you, who is more to you than seven sons, has given birth to him." Then Naomi took the child and laid him on her lap and became his nurse. And the women of the neighborhood gave him a name, saying, "A son has been born to Naomi." They named him Obed. He was the father of Jesse, the father of David.*

Now look specifically for what titles the women bestow on our Lord in their declaration above.

Oh sweet, beautiful redemption! He has not left you. You may be looking backwards at all Christ has done and rejoicing alongside Ruth and Naomi or you may be in the thick of the struggle and all you can do is raise your hands to the heavens and ask for restoration, for nourishment, for a reminder the life comes anew. Where ever you are, know this...

He sent a Redeemer, through the line of David, at just the right time.

He is restoring and working and nourishing you.

He redeems situations and relationships and people at just the right time.

Entrust all of life to Him, your blessed, beautiful Kinsman-Redeemer.

Exploration
You are redeemed. What relationships or situations are you asking God to redeem currently? Maybe it's just a cruddy day, maybe it's a job, a family situation, a prodigal child, your health. He is in it. He is working!

Write a prayer giving all your concerns for this relationship or situation to the Lord today, our at-just-the-right-time Redeemer.

he calls me clay

Isaiah 43:4a
Because you are precious in my eyes,
and honored, and I love you…

week five
He Calls Me Clay

Right Where We Belong
Clay Loves, Clay Understands
Clay Walks
Clay Fades
Clay Accepts: My Purposes, His Plans

heart verse

But now, O Lord, you are our Father;
we are the clay, and you are our potter;
we are all the work of your hand.
Isaiah 64:8

he calls me clay
▼ ▼ ▼ ▼

day one
Right Where We Belong

Midweek is back in session at church, and while I'm excited to see the faith growth it will bring to my children, it really means one thing for me...*Daniel Tiger* night. Judge me if you will, but I really love this one-hour time slot when I get to curl up on the couch with my smallest child, snuggle, and hear life's problems solved from the vantage point of an animated talking tiger and his family.

Last Wednesday, Zeke and I were happily watching our favorite tiger family pick multiple kinds of fruit in an animated garden when the show switched to a montage of a live-action family intended to drive home whatever the lesson was of the night. This was all well and good until… the family on the screen started mixing play-dough colors.

I kid you not, there was serious color mixing going on, with parental approval! They were making some kind of pizza with a pink bottom and green, red, yellow, and white bits of toppings.

The preschool- aged child was happily pushing the colored bits as far into the play-dough crust as it would go, and all I could think was "AHHHHHHHHH, it's never going to come apart! Don't do it. Just don't do it. You are well on your way to molding brown play-dough. Who wants brown play-dough? What are these parents thinking??!!"

At that moment, Zeke looks at me and says, completely unaware of my inner dialogue of judgment, "Ooooo – they're making rainbow play-dough."

My perspective was instantly opened.

These children, this family, was making something. They were making something pretty. They were making something that felt good, something crafted by their own two hands, no, their own six hands together. That's what Zeke saw, when all I saw was a mess.

So often, our perspective is very narrow when compared to God's.

I look around and I see mess.

He sees molding and shaping, crafting and creating.

Please open your Bible and read Isaiah 64:1-8. Which titles for God are found in verse 8?

What title does He give to us in Isaiah 64:8?

Imagine God, coming down from the mountains, to be part of your life. He doesn't *have* to engage. He doesn't *need* us. He is God. But He values relationship in a way that I'm not even sure we can fully comprehend. One of His primary attributes is omnipresence. He can be everywhere at one time. Many of us know this as a nice theological idea, but don't miss the personal context of it. He is present. He comes down. What does the writer beg God to do in Isaiah 64:1-8, which we just read?

God deigned to create the universe and walk in the garden with Adam and Eve. He came down from heaven to walk our soil as Jesus Christ, God made flesh. He is present. He sent His Spirit to live and dwell among us, God in our hearts and lives and homes. He is present. He will come back and restore this Earth and me and all Creation to perfection. *He is present.*

The message of our passage in Isaiah 64 is not only are we made and formed by God but...

We are held by God.

Write out Isaiah 64:8 below to focus your mind and heart on his work in you and for you.

Potter and Maker means the one who is crafting and holding the pot, shaping and forming, constantly. We want a bright neon sign with solar panels and flashing lights to point us to God. We want trumpets and angel choirs, and something bigger and better than our current situation, but that's not His style generally speaking. Potter and Clay is His style, Isaiah tells us. Often, we might not see Him, because He is holding us, shaping us. He *can* do signs and angel choirs, but He definitely holds us in His hands. He holds us in the tight grip of His grace and He's not finished with us.

This week, as we discover how we ourselves are *clay* held in the Potter's hands, being shaped and formed, we will also see how God teaches as the Potter, how He instructs us in our purposes and forms us as His vessels. We'll also see what glory there is in the very basic act of letting Him mix us up like play-dough. God forms rainbows of beauty where we thought it was all just leading to muddy brown.

For today, focus on this:

"We are all the work of your hand..."

This proclamation in Isaiah 64:8 means we are all *currently* the work of His hands. We were His work when he created us. We will be the work of His hands when we are in heaven with Him, and we are the work of His hands today…this day. You are a beautiful lump of rainbow-colored-playdough, held in the palm of His hands.

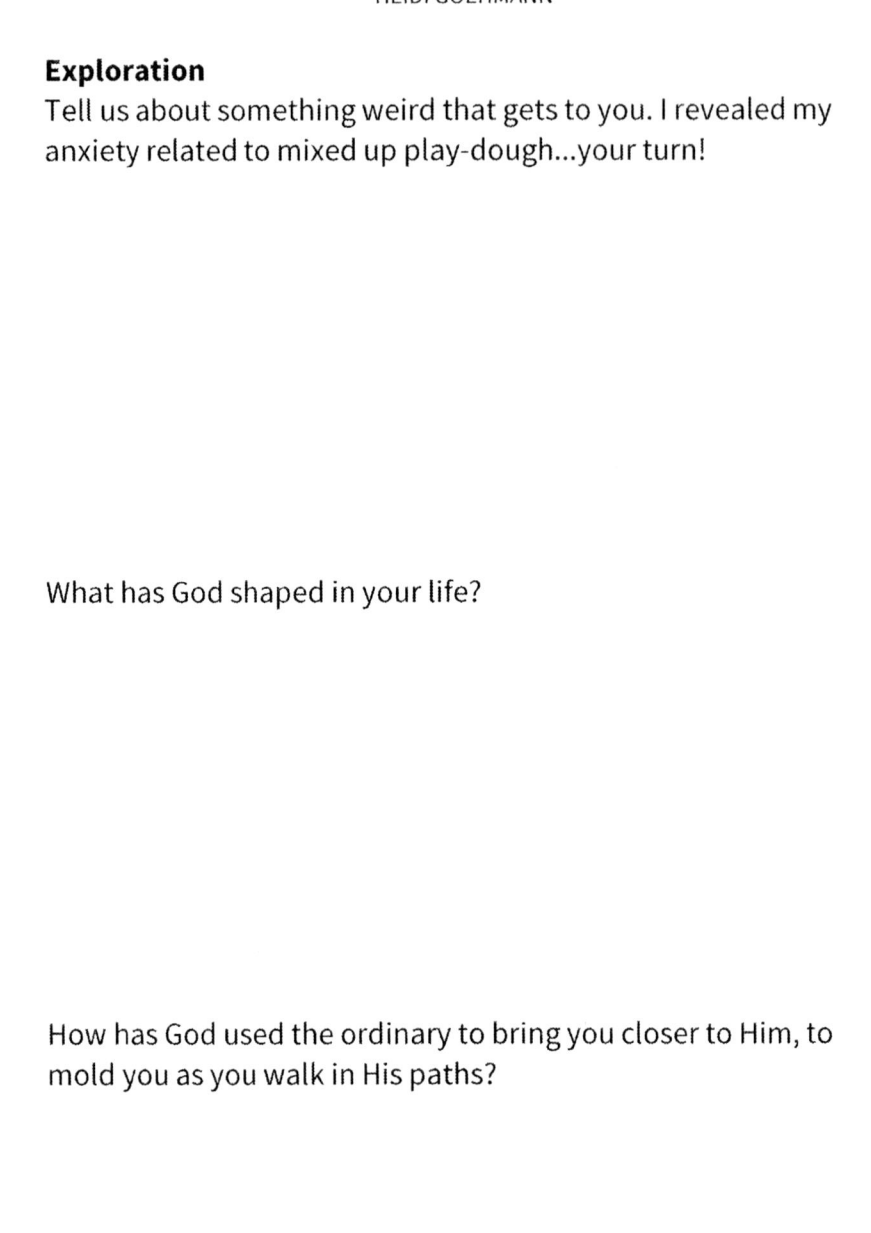

Exploration
Tell us about something weird that gets to you. I revealed my anxiety related to mixed up play-dough...your turn!

What has God shaped in your life?

How has God used the ordinary to bring you closer to Him, to mold you as you walk in His paths?

he calls me clay
▼ ▼ ▼ ▼

day two
Clay Loves, Clay Understands

There are things in this life that people try to explain to me that I don't think I will ever understand. For instance, how radio waves allow sound to travel to my car stereo. Really, anything beyond the very basic laws of physics - nope, don't understand it. I like to look at and contemplate abstract art, but for the most part, you could explain it to me all the live-long day, but I would still probably miss the point intended, most times.

I've made peace with my lack of knowledge on all things. At 30-something years old, I'm just old enough to know that life is short, and young enough to still be going full throttle. While I want to understand things, I can accurately identify when to say, "I'm so thankful other people understand that. Thank you, Lord, for the diversity of the human mind."

Sometimes it's ok to be perplexed. It can be really good actually, if you approach it from a slightly different angle. When something is beyond our understanding, it serves to remind us there is something bigger than us, that we don't know everything, nor are we intended to. It means that we need each other, and one another's gifts. It means that God is God in His courts, and He alone knows all things.

Today, we will learn that in making us as clay, God has crafted us within His own design. He created a particular art to understanding for humans and there is freedom in that.

Please read Isaiah 29:15-19 in your Bible. What does this passage say about our understanding?

So often in this world, we want to be the potter and not the clay.

We want to *know*, but on our own time, our own topics, in our own place. We are the hiders from the Lord's counsel (Isaiah 29:15). We think we know, when really we do not. We turn things upside down.

Look up the following supportive passages to these statements. What picture of wisdom and understanding do each of these passages give you?

Proverbs 1:7

1 Corinthians 1:25

Colossians 2:2-3

God does open our eyes and our ears, our hearts, and our minds. He is our Potter, and He works the clay and turns the wheel in ways we least expect. Colossians 2:2-3 gives us an important perspective on how we receive understanding from knowledge. It does not only tell us that we receive understanding from knowledge and facts, but that we will receive understanding *from encouragement and unity and love.*

The picture given to us in Isaiah 29:17 is that of a fruitful field. Our fruits are encouragement, unity, love and more.

Isaiah 29:19 tells us we obtain fresh joy from the Lord.

Something special happens when we open the Scriptures. When we dare to open this book. We will find knowledge, understanding, yes, as well as the encouragement we need for the day, reminders of God's love for us and strength to love our neighbor, guidance and the Spirit's work towards family unity.

All because we opened The Word.

When we come together in community around the Word there is no understanding quite like it. God opens minds and God alone. Drugs are created and healing happens because God ordained it. Radio waves collect together across space and do whatever they do because God wants us to hear. Art becomes art because we were gifted with vision and color and talent from a Creative God. But no wisdom, no understanding is quite as magical as the beauty of the blind seeing and the deaf hearing because the people of God gathered round to hear the words of the Bible. This brings us out of darkness into the light of understanding.

Hear it from Isaiah 29:18 again:

> *In that day the deaf shall hear*
> *the words of a book,*
> *and out of their gloom and darkness*
> *the eyes of the blind shall see.*

What area of your life do you need wisdom for today? Add your requests to the prayer below:

Lord, open our eyes, open our ears to Your wisdom. Give us hearts that are encouraged and minds that fire neurons that are continuously growing in You. You, oh Father, are our Potter. You, Jesus, mold us in Your image every day. Spirit, grant that our knowledge would always be accompanied by the Love and Unity with Your people. Lord, help us. May what we learn and grow in always glorify You and lead us in Your truth, as well as lead others to Salvation in Your Word. Lord, please give me wisdom for…

In Jesus' name we pray, by the power of the good and gracious Holy Spirit. Amen.

Exploration
What leaves you perplexed in this world?

What connection do you see between knowledge, understanding, and love?

Consider for a moment, how does God work understanding when people study the Bible together or offer one another Christian wisdom?

he calls me clay
▼ ▼ ▼ ▼

day three
Clay Walks

Are the pages of Isaiah getting easier to turn as we man-handle them? Is it easier to find the Bible app on your phone?

My study Bible has these ridiculously thin pages and until a section has been tossed and turned again and again, I trip, with giant thumbs, trying to find the right chapter and verse. The pages stick together. I turn them and go six chapters too far. I back track and finally land on the selected passage. It becomes easier as I turn the pages more and more. As I study more, the pages have my fingerprints all over them. A side effect of this is that the pages get just crinkly enough that I can turn them deftly and without all the frustration.

This is how faith seems to work as well.

Turn to Isaiah 30:18-22 today. What insight about faith can you glean there?

God walks with us as our fingers move across the pages of our Bibles. Walking is one of the primary descriptors used for faith in the Bible. In Isaiah 30, we find a fun name for God associated with this walk. He is our Teacher.

We do not walk alone. We have a Teacher who guides and leads. While this passage doesn't speak about clay, it fits into our title of clay because clay is moldable. It's instruct-able. When we say, "Mold me and make me, Lord. You are the Potter, I am the clay," we also say –

Teach me.

Walk with me.

Show me the way.

Isaiah 30 gives us clarity in this picture of walking with our Lord. As we walk in faith – *not in perfection*, but in the simple walking with and by the strength of the Spirit – we grow up into Him, into the Teacher, Christ Jesus. Look at Ephesians 4:14-15 and 5:1-2. What connections can you find in these verses between truth, love, and walking?

Therefore...walk in love. (from Ephesians 5:1-2)

I so often walk in hurt, in bitterness, in impatience, in discontent, in annoyance, and in apathy.

Because of Jesus Christ, I can walk in the love He has for me and all those people around me. I am instruct-able. I need and I have a Teacher to show me the way, to walk beside me, to walk behind me and to cover me in forgiveness when I mess up. He also walks ahead to guide me in the True Light.

When I learn, I'm walking. When I grow, I'm walking. When I trust, I'm walking.

Check out Acts 9:1-2. What position or relationship did Paul originally have with the early church?

Yet, Paul was walking as God's clay before he even knew it. He *was* walking hunting down people in persecution. He *was* walking in destruction, but in this very experience, as Paul was literally walking to destroy, God show Him *The Way*. Christianity is referenced here and only here in Scriptures as "the Way." Jesus is The Way and our job as the Church is only to point to Him, to walk so people can see Him. Paul walked that road to Damascus and his life changed forever. Jesus made His way plain. With Jesus, Paul walked in Life and Forgiveness, then and He walks it in eternity now.

Just like Paul, when I am wrong, I'm walking and Jesus sees. When I repent, I'm walking and Jesus hears. When the breath of Christ's forgiveness rushes in and covers my sin, I'm walking and He shapes and molds.

Christ Jesus leads, even when we have no clue. I walk, by His gifts, in His love and in His mercy. I walk through crinkly pages and brokenness into marvelous, inestimable Grace.

Keep walking, friend. Clay walks.

Exploration
What was your first experience with studying the Bible?

What group Bible studies have been memorable for you?

What is the hardest part of walking in love for you?

he calls me clay
▼ ▼ ▼

day four
Clay Fades

Some days I feel like I'm fading fast. I just sent a text to my friend that said, "My schedule is overwhelming. I know I need to give something up. Something has to give, but what?"

Do you ever feel like that? What kinds of activities and commitments stretch your schedule?

Some of you may be nodding and whispering something like, "Every day. I feel stretched every day."

The reality is that we *are* fading. We can't do everything. We can only charge ahead at 100% for so long. We will absolutely burn out. Even with the Holy Spirit dwelling inside of us, we were created for rest, just as we were created for work.

Part of my problem, and I'm guessing this resonates with many of you, is that I'm trying to keep it all together for so many people. I think I'm the glue that holds our life together and if I fall apart, or even if I take a nap, who in the world will keep everyone standing? (And seriously, if I do take a nap, Living Room Armageddon appears to take place.)

This is one thing I have learned through my study of God's character:

There is a difference between being all things to all people, and believing people need me to be all things for them.

The first — being all things to all people — a concept Paul teaches in 1 Corinthians 9:22, is living in hope, being willing to share hope, and to share the way God has worked in my life within the opportunities He gives me. The second begins and ends in a belief that God can't do it without me. We get trapped in the not-quite-conscious belief that He can't use someone else. We want to be needed by God. He uses me, yes, but He surely doesn't need me.

Why am I so busy trying to be God?

It's important for me to understand that clay fades. I am dispensable. I would be missed on this earth, but I'm not the only one He can use.

Let's read Isaiah 40:18-24 to get a better handle on the difference between God needing us and God using us. While you read Isaiah 40:18-24, list all the things in the passage that give a nod to God's greatness.

Building idols isn't always about gold and silver. We make an idol of ourselves when we think we are so very necessary to everyone's existence. We puff ourselves up, saying by our actions, "What would they do without me? Aren't I so busy and important? This place would fall apart without me."

Deep down we are afraid to fade. We are afraid that we won't have a legacy, we won't be remembered, *we won't matter.*

Without intending to, we build little cracked idols of wood and peeling gold by trying to be everything for our homes, our families, our employers, our churches, and our friends.

God would never have us forsake relationships or dishonor our commitments, but the question becomes -

What is at the center of these relationships and commitments?

>How do we put our children *at the center* instead of God?
>How do we put our marriages and our spouses *at the center* instead of God?
>How do we put our homes and our household chores *at the center* instead of God?
>How do we put our vocations and our successes *at the center* instead of God?
>How do we put our sports teams and our hobbies and our interests *at the center* instead of God?

When you look at this list, which area of your life do you think you struggle to keep God at the center of most?

These are all things we literally "build" our life around.

Read Isaiah 40:24 again below and circle any words that acknowledge the results of building these idols.

> *Scarcely are they planted, scarcely sown,*
>   *scarcely has their stem taken root in the earth,*
> *when he blows on them, and they wither,*
>   *and the tempest carries them off like stubble.*

Clay fades is actually good news. The world gives pressure. It says, "Hold it together. Hold everything together." We know it's not sustainable. We can feel it slipping from our grasp.

Clay does fade.

We only last so long here on this earth and we were never meant to hold everything together; only God was.

So, when you need a moment, take a moment. In that moment, place it all at His feet.

Worship Him. My prayer in this moment sounds like, "You know I can't do this, Lord. Only You can hold it all together. Only You. I am Clay."

I am Clay.
I can't do it all.
Only you can, Lord.

Take this burden, Lord. Take it.

Jesus promises that He does carry them as He walks alongside us. After all, what is the promise of Matthew 11:28-30?

He holds all of the pieces. He holds our life and our children, our homes and our jobs, our health, all of it in His hands. He hands us an easier yoke, a Salvation-shaped yoke of peace and joy and forgiveness and love unending.

**I am clay.
I can't do it all.
Only you can, Lord.**

So, if you find yourself, sitting like me…spent, tired, wondering what's going to give…take this truth and write it somewhere. Then place it somewhere prominent. Share it with a friend who could use it. Share the struggle of the journey together.

Exploration
What kinds of things push you to the end of your rope? Your job, cleaning, cooking, family drama, etc?

What is your favorite way to turn things over to God? Do you have a favorite prayer or song, verse, or refrain that helps you place the burdens of life back on Your Savior?

he calls me clay
▼ ▼ ▼ ▼

day five
Clay Accepts: My Purposes, His Plans

If you pictured yourself as a clay vessel, formed by God, what kind do you think you would be — a cup, a mug, a vase, a bowl? What do you imagine the potter forming you into? It's a fun question! Share your answer in words or pictures here:

The Biblical picture of clay reminds us that we don't all look the same. We all have different shapes and sizes, colors and bumps. Perhaps most importantly, we have different purposes. Sometimes I like those purposes. Sometimes I'm in love with those purposes. Other times I'd like to take those purposes and shove 'em.

God addresses the issue of my jaded heart in Isaiah 45:9-11. What is the source of all the woes in this passage?

Let's be honest for a moment. Below, you'll see that I rephrased the Biblical questions to express the similar ones I think we ask internally in our own lives. Underneath each one, write how you would phrase them.

Does the clay say to the pot? How often do I say to God: what in the world are You doing?

Your work has no handles? Are you sure you're doing this right, God? I think it might be better if you gave me this or we went over here and did this instead.

What are you begetting? Why? Why? Why, God?

With what are you in labor? What are we making here...it better be something worthwhile, God.

The Israelites' hearts at the time of Isaiah could be pretty hard, but ours can, too. As soon as I think I'm all over this spiritual maturity thing, life happens. I learn pretty quickly that I'm clay, wanting handles when I'm meant to be a bowl.

The problem isn't our questions, really, it's the hardness, the "I know better than You, God" attitude or the "My ways are better than Yours, God" attitude.

Jesus instructs toward a different posture in Matthew 7:7-8. Why do you think this posture makes such a difference?

We still get to ask questions, we still get to come to God because of all Jesus did and who He is, but we do so knowing that His ways are better. His ways are Life and Salvation. His ways are True and Honorable and Lovely and Just.

There's another passage about our life as a pot or jar of clay. Look at 2 Corinthians 4:6-9. What pressure does clay undergo in the making? What pressures do we undergo?

What promises of God can you find in these same verses?

God's light has shone in our hearts. They're different because of Jesus. We are bearers of Christ's message in everything we have and everything we do and every single purpose we fulfill, no matter what life looks like. When things happen in our lives and our steps seem unsure, we rest in the Potter. Our security is in the "knowledge of the glory of God *in the face of Jesus Christ.*" Isn't that beautiful? I'd really rather be Jesus's face to someone than my own, wouldn't you?

Isaiah 45 is actually about a guy named Cyrus and some stubborn people, but it bleeds God's promises across the page in a way that reaches us in the 21st century beautifully. Cyrus would be the king who would free the Israelites and return them to their homeland after a long exile. Most of the Israelites at that time hadn't ever seen the land of Israel, but their love of it, their place in it was handed down from one generation to another. Still, many of the Israelites were resistant to the plan to return home, to return to Israel. They liked their own lives, even though it was technically captivity. Babylon was a nice place, a comfortable place. Never mind the bondage and all that, it was cozy.

Sound familiar? I really like cozy. Sometimes when God asks for us to get un-cozy, the best thing we can do is let the Holy Spirit remind us of His promises. Turn back to Isaiah 45:1-8, the portion preceding the verses we read earlier in this lesson. What promise does God give to Cyrus in Isaiah 45:1-2, 5-6?

God opens doors. That's who He is. And He levels the road we walk on. He promises to equip His jars of clay, and He does. Along the way, He opens our hearts to His Word, His people, and His work.

What doors has God opened for you in the past? What uncomfortable thing has He brought you through into the light of the "knowledge of the glory of God in the face of Christ"?

How do you see things in your life differently through the message of Christ Jesus?

Any questions we have along the journey of life are good. They help us to know the Potter. Let us not tell Him what we think He should do with the wheel, however. *Ask away, but let Him mold.* You are a treasured vessel, lovingly created and formed from the beginning and each day since. Entrust it all to Him, who molds and makes.

Exploration
End today by sharing some questions you have for God in the space below. Use a litany of "You are the potter. I am the clay." after each thing you write down.

he calls me sought out

Ecclesiastes *Isaiah 43:4a*
*Because you are precious in my eyes,
and honored, and I love you...*

week six

He Calls Me Sought Out

You are Never Forsaken
The Gut Punch of Left Alone
Politics, History Class, Alpha and Omega
Earthquakes, Prayers, and Prophecy
Silencing My Own White Noise

heart verse:
*And they shall be called The Holy People,
The Redeemed of the* L{\small ORD}*;
and you shall be called Sought Out,
A City Not Forsaken.
Isaiah 62:12*

he calls me sought out
▼ ▼ ▼ ▼

day one
You are Never Forsaken

Have you ever loaned out a book and never received it back? That's annoying, right? Or maybe you've been on the other end and stopped borrowing books from friends because a borrowed book is as good as lost in your house? What is it with loaned books? We return them to the library, but if a friend loans us a book it suddenly goes MIA overnight. I have been on both the receiving and the losing end of this strange book conundrum.

I have one book I loan out frequently. I hand it out like a grandma hands out butterscotch candies, just waiting for their rightful recipient in the bottom of her purse for a good three years. Each time I loan it out, I don't care if I ever get this it back. For this particular book, it's that important to me that people read it. (Shhhhh. Don't tell anyone. It'll be our secret.) I may keep Amazon in business with the number of copies I have bought and "lost" to people over the years. But in the end, who cares?

The message of this book is so powerful for me, that I press it on people,
"You must read it."
"It's life changing."
"Let me send it to you."

What is the message of the book? The same as the one we hear in our passage from Isaiah today. Please read Isaiah 62:10-12 and circle the following titles as you come to them in the verse below or in your Bible — Holy, Redeemed, Sought Out, and Not Forsaken.

> Go through, go through the gates;
>   prepare the way for the people;
> build up, build up the highway;
>   clear it of stones;
>   lift up a signal over the peoples.
> Behold, the Lord has proclaimed
>   to the end of the earth:
> Say to the daughter of Zion,
>   "Behold, your salvation comes;
> behold, his reward is with him,
>   and his recompense before him."
> And they shall be called The Holy People,
>   The Redeemed of the Lord
> and you shall be called Sought Out,
>   A City Not Forsaken.

The book mentioned earlier is a historical retelling of the message, life, and writings of the prophet Hosea, a contemporary of the prophet Isaiah. Their messages overlap and are in concordance with one another; but just as each of us have a different testimony of Christ written through our lives, so does the work and words of each prophet. It's helpful to dig into them side by side when we get the opportunity.

Hosea has something to say about *Sought Out*. My personal opinion is that His message of sought out, of not forsaken, is stronger than any other Biblical book, but maybe that's just because my book found me at the right place, at the right time, with a message I needed to know more than any other:

You are sought out.

You are not forsaken.

This is the message of redemption, of the Holy One not only coming to us in His Son and His Word, but seeking us out, searching our hearts and our lives until He gets hold of us, literally *chasing us down* with His Son and His Word.

Read the following verses from Hosea to piece together his story. After each passage reference, write what details you find there about Hosea, the story of his family, and of God's great forgiveness working through all of it:

Hosea 1:2-3

Hosea 3:1-3

Hosea 6:1-3

Sometimes, I need to know that *at my worst*, I am sought out. The message of *Sought Out* is what brings me up from the ash heap. It brings me back from ugly sin and creating messes wherever I travel. It finally shuts my mouth when words are flying left and right, and edification is far from my heart and mind. What does 1 Timothy 1:15 have to say about our worst?

He died for you and me and Gomer and Israel, *at our worst.*

Read Isaiah 62:12 again, as well as Isaiah 63:1, both written out below. Remember, there's no chapter and verse numbers in the original Hebrew. It is a fluid passage. Underline or circle the words most closely associated with salvation for you. In the margin, share why you chose these words.

> *And they shall be called The Holy People,*
>   *The Redeemed of the* Lord;
> *and you shall be called Sought Out,*
>   *A City Not Forsaken.*
> *Who is this who comes from Edom,*
>   *in crimsoned garments from Bozrah,*
> *he who is splendid in his apparel,*
>   *marching in the greatness of his strength?*
> *"It is I, speaking in righteousness,*
>   *mighty to save."*

He is many things, not the least of which is...
He is mighty to seek, mighty to save.

God's message of *Sought Out* is also the message that you are worthy of saving, worthy of seeking, finding, and showering with Grace, not because you look like you have it together, but because you don't.

Hosea loved in the hardest circumstances, in unimaginable grace and mercy. He sought out his wife maybe because she was just that precious to him, but definitely because God told Him to. That is the kind of God our Trinity God is — Father, Son, and Holy Spirit. Our God seeks in places you and I wouldn't even think of salvation going.

He is mighty to save. You are Sought Out.

*My lend-to-as-many-people-as-I-can book is Redeeming Love by Francine Rivers. Check it out at your local library or where books are sold.

Exploration
In our culture, "I'm not worthwhile" or "I'm not enough" is a difficult lie of Satan for people to overcome. What message would you share with a friend struggling with not being good enough for Jesus or not good enough in their roles as employee, wife, mom, student, etc?

What "least of these" people do you have a heart for?

When has God ministered to you and sought you out or hunted you down to show you His grace?

he calls me sought out
▼ ▼ ▼ ▼

day two
The Gut Punch of Left Alone

Alone sounds so good to me as I write this. As a mom of four kids, therapist, and pastor's wife, I love me some alone time. Give me a cup of coffee and a good book, a glass of wine and a fire in my backyard, or a bathtub and a cup of earl grey, and it's like a tiny window of heaven. Alone time is a precious resource around my house.

But I also know what it means to feel truly alone, as in *left alone*...and there's a big difference between these two scenarios.

Have you had that moment? That moment when it feels like everyone has walked away. Maybe a loss has left you wondering who will fill the gap— the loss of their touch, their laughter, wondering who else will share your secrets. Maybe you have been left by a loved one, a father, a mother, a husband, a brother – someone who walked out the door leaving you behind with the tears, the shock, and the anger. Or maybe you have been left standing to face the bullies of life, and when you looked around, not a single person stayed to fight alongside you.

Whether in little or in the big moments of life, we have all experienced the stomach drop of *left alone*.

A wise therapist I know is fond of saying, "There are two sides to every coin." Today, let's return to Isaiah 62:12, our passage from yesterday, and remind ourselves of the titles bestowed on us by Christ, once again. There is so much in this snippet of Scripture. Please read Isaiah 62:12 and write the titles you find within it to refresh your memory.

One side of the coin is being *Sought Out*, being chosen and loved, someone running after us. The other side of the coin here is to know what *Not Forsaken* looks like, we need to experience left alone.

Words associated with *forsaken* in the dictionary include: abandon, desert, disown, renounce, refuse, or discard.

This is often the world's message to us – "you aren't worth the time or energy, you aren't important enough, you are insignificant."

This is never, ever God's message to us.

Flip the coin again and remember Who Jesus is and let His voice be louder than the world's today:

Sought out means not forsaken, not abandoned, not disowned, not renounced, not refused, and never, never discarded.

Look up the following verses and write what you hear in each of God's message for you of *Not Forsaken*:
Deuteronomy 31:8

1 Chronicles 28:20

2 Corinthians 4:9-10

Hebrews 13:5-6

We may undergo trial. There may be good days and bad days and rotten days and complacent days and joy-filled days and everything-in-between days, but there will never be *forsaken* days.

You are *Not Forsaken*. It is your name, placed on you by God Himself. Notice the capital letters in the Isaiah text — Sought Out, Not Forsaken. He will be with you each day, in the wonderful and in the hard. Cling to that. Let it seep into your soul.

You are not forsaken.

Exploration

Martin Luther and other commentators apply this verse also to the Church on earth — *the Church* being the followers of Christ here and now, and across history. How has God sought out His people in history?

What historical moments come to mind when you consider that the Church is not forsaken?

What promise of the future is there for the Church in *Not Forsaken* and *Sought Out*?

> The church's one foundation is Jesus Christ, her Lord;
> she is his new creation by water and the Word.
> From heaven he came and sought her to be his holy bride;
> with his own blood he bought her, and for her life he died.
> (public domain[viii])

he calls me sought out

▼ ▼ ▼ ▼

day three
Politics, History Class, Alpha and Omega

History is our friend Karl's passion. You get him started and he could pretty much go on forever, recounting vengeful and valiant leaders, epic battles, and the contribution of those left unmentioned in the texts of history books. Karl's version of history is my favorite. It's passionate, but purposeful. Everything he shares is spirited and he makes you hungry to know more, hear more, and learn more. Better than that, in almost every circumstance, he makes you hungry for God. Karl teaches at a State University, so I'm sure his classroom looks a little bit different, but in private conversation and in teaching at church, Karl is on fire with a message. He lays out history in a way that makes you stand in awe of a God who holds all of it in His hands, from the beginning to the messy middle to our Savior's faithfulness each day we have yet to travel.

Isaiah shares a similar message with just as much zeal in Isaiah 44:6-8. Let's open our Bibles and read that text. What in this passage stands out to you as particularly speaking of zeal and zealousness?

What a great apologetics question from God Himself -

"Who is like me?"

Is there another God like Him? No, He is the First and the Last…and everything in between.

God sat on His throne and created humankind. He created every flower and every tree. He set the planets in motion. Countries and constitutions sprang up, kingdoms and territories came to be, and God was God over all of it. Wars have been fought, lives lost, and yet, His faithfulness continues. New nations form, cultures live and grow, languages develop. Disasters come upon the Earth, dictators oppress, and God's heart breaks. Still, He sees the bigger plan unfolding. To us, it is like the slow unrolling of a tapestry. To Him, it's the blink of an eye, a piece of all eternity.

He is the First and the Last, and everything in between.

Humankind makes gods out of idols and builds temples made by human hands. We chase wealth and power and success. We destroy one another to be the best, be the biggest, be the greatest, when we were never intended for those purposes. Through all of it, God raises up faithful ones. God leads His people from ancient times (v. 7), appointed for *His* purposes, setting them apart for Kingdom work. The wheels of the clock turn, time marches on, the Word goes out into the world, and the message of Christ's life-giving sacrifice and resurrection never changes.

Fill in the missing words from Isaiah 44:6 below:

> *Thus says the Lord, the King of Israel*
> *and his Redeemer, the Lord of hosts:*
> *"I am the first and I am the last;*
>
> *_____ _____ there is*
>
> *_____ _____.*

God alone sits on the throne. We think we have all this power and authority. We think the next presidential election or stock market crash will make or break mankind. It may break a nation, but it will not break us. It will not break His message, His Spirit, or His Word. Through the sands of time, the Word continues to go out, leading people to Him in the dark and in the light of life, in the triumph and in the defeat, in the famine and when there's plenty.

We are simply witnesses.

He is the First and the Last, and everything in between.

We are called to declare His purposes. That is all. Like our friend Karl, may our message always be of the hidden things, the works done faithfully, rarely written in textbooks. When we witness from the vantage point of believers in a faithful God, nothing is lost in the drama, every bit of the tumult and the turmoil has a purpose. As cheesy as it sounds, it really is His story anyway.

What is the response to the hypothetical question *"Is there a God besides me?"* in Isaiah 44:8? Write it below.

Scripture has a lot more to say about God as *the Rock*. Look up the following verses and identify the promises in each of God, as our Rock.

Psalm 18:2

Psalm 31:3

Psalm 62:6-7

Luke 6:47-48

I don't want to know any other gods, Lord. I want to follow You. I don't want to trust in anything else, Lord. I want to follow You. I want to see You in every piece of history, every trial and every glory. Be my Rock. Be my Fortress. Be my Defender, and let me never look to another person, thing, idea, or place to provide that for me. *Only You, Lord. Only You.*

He is the First and the Last and everything in between.

Exploration
The book of Revelation really has a lot to say on this subject. Check out the following four verses for further reflection that He really is the first and the last and all the stuff in the middle too.

Rev. 1:8

Rev. 1:17-18

Rev. 21:6-7

Rev. 22:13

Why do you think the book of Revelation returns to this concept again and again?

he calls me sought out
▼▼▼▼

day four
Earthquakes, Prayers, and Prophecy

I have been through two earthquakes in my life. They were tiny, but there is something unsettling about the earth shaking beneath your feet. As a child, when the first one happened, I was shocked and unsure. I had nightmares for weeks. If the Earth could shake, what else could happen? What we experienced was little, but would another one come and swallow my family up? My parents comforted my fears brought on by an overactive imagination with incredible patience.

The next one happened shortly after Dave and I were married. I was an adult. Things should be better, right? Life should maybe feel a little firmer as an adult? That earthquake stuck with me for weeks, months even. It opened questions long left tucked away. If the ground itself moved while we went about our business, how unstable was this fragile thing called life?

Yesterday we had the Rock standing strong, today we have mountains quaking. Open your Bible to Isaiah 64:1-5. How do the messages of the Rock we know is Christ and the earthquake shaking us meet?

Did you notice the irony? These Israelites *are asking* for an earthquake. They want the mountains to tremble if it means God would come to meet with them. What I called instability, what created fear in my heart and soul, these people were desperate for, because it represented the mighty act of a God that they thought was all but lost. What was their solution to desperation?

These verses and those that follow are a prayer of confession — repentance and reconnection with a God they loved and forgot they longed for. In His absence, or rather in the lifting of His closeness, they found themselves parched, thirsty, and incomplete.

"We long for Your presence, Lord!" is their song. "We need You, Lord. We looked away. Forgive us in Your great mercy, we cry out. Make the mountains shake with Your power and might and *Here*-ness."

And God answers. He answers prayers — He comes here.

Jesus Christ came down from on High to be present with His people, and there were literal earthquakes.

What was the event that caused the first in Matthew 27:50-52?

The second earthquake is recorded in Matthew 28:1-2. What event is the cause found in these verses?

He causes the earth to shake, the foundations to tremble because He, friends, is the True Foundation. He is the only thing we really have to stand on.

Want to see another earthquake? Just one more? Turn the pages of Scripture to Acts 4:23-31. What details accompany the event of the earthquake this time?

Prayer does crazy things. God does crazy things. His power is not of this world and when we pray, stuff happens — namely, loving tender care in relationship with a loving tender God. The earth may not shake when we pray. It could, but even when it doesn't, earth shaking things happen in our life because we are molded and shaped by His Spirit instead of our own will.

He is ALIVE. His Spirit is at work! I would rather lean on that any day, rather than the floor underneath me that trembles like leaves falling from a tree.

And so we pray...
Lord, make my earth quake with Your presence. Let not my heart trust in anything but You and You alone. We call upon You. We confess our trust in the things of this world, in the foundations of this temporal place that passes away. We look to You, Lord, and

the forgiveness You offer. We thank You for Your Grace and Mercy and work in our lives daily, for seeking us out and bringing us to You, Lord. Thank You for Your Faithfulness every day. In Jesus's name we pray. Amen.

Write your own additions to the prayer in the margins. He is steady always, our God — Father, Savior, and Counselor.

Exploration
Have you ever been through a small or large natural disaster? What was your experience?

What comfort does it give, knowing that God sent His Spirit into your life and you will never be without His presence?

Do you have an example of when Jesus shook your life up, metaphorically (or literally!), and you drew closer to Him because of it? Your example may be just the witness that someone else needs to hear! Share a few thoughts about a time you were shook up.

he calls me sought out

▼ ▼ ▼ ▼

day five
Silencing My Own White Noise

The world is noisy.

I like noise for the most part. I like energy and life running around me. Small children wailing mean they are fighting to be heard, protests for injustice are right up my alley, and concerts with giant speakers and loud praise do not offend me in the least. What I don't like is white noise. I don't like prittle-prattle, grumbling, and listening to the sound of my own voice for too long. My children know that 18 (out of 75) is a completely reasonable TV volume setting and not a notch higher. My phone alarm is barely audible, and Dave once bought one of those gurgling rock fountains at a yard sale and I delivered it to his office instead. Marriage saved.

So much of the noise in our world is meaningless. It sounds harsh, even judgmental, but please hear me differently: I can only take so much. *We* can only take so much.

So many opinions to sort though, so much news channel babble, so many ads vying for us to buy stuff — eat this, do this, look like this...

God talks about trying to get our attention in the middle of all this in Isaiah 65. Let's look at Isaiah 65:1-2. What do these verses have to say about all the white noise?

God doesn't just seek us. He fights for us. He's jumping up and down with the neon signs of creation and the miracle of life and the gift of restoration, while we give all of our attention to fuzzy TV screens and spotty reception.

He says, "Here I am, Here I am."

How often do we miss Him in the day-to-day of life because of all the other voices we are filtering Him through? What ways do you combat these attempts to grab your attention from things other than Jesus?

Then there is the internal white noise. This noise is worse, in my opinion. The internal shame voice of "not enough" — not good enough, not smart enough, not pretty enough. I think I repeat it over and over again and you might be tired of me saying it, but I am convinced we have to say it until our internal selves get it. This voice is not of God. This is the voice of the Devil telling you lies. The Father of Lies, himself, berating you for never living up, never reaching out, never saying it right.

In the strain, there is the internal voice of selfishness that says, "I need, I want, I deserve." There's greed, which says, "Those people have more. I need more. How do I get more?" And the voice of discontent saying, "My life is mediocre. I'm not like them. Why isn't God intervening the way I'd like?"

Even the church has its own white noise, external and internal voices that put aside the Truth of the Word, prefer rules over mercy, and make hierarchies for grace. There are a million distractions from the objective of loving our God and loving our neighbor, justice and love going out, and bringing the message of restoration to the world.

BE QUIET, voices!

The beautiful thing is that God addresses this battle, this battle against powers and principalities that looks a lot like static and distraction all around.

What battle gear does God give us in Ephesians 6:10-18?

Put on the whole armor. Strap it on. It's all richly supplied by God. We have a different wardrobe from the world. We have a different vantage point through that Helmet of Salvation. We are given tools that block out the white noise, that provide a filter. Let's use them!

Now, believing that Scripture interprets Scripture, look at Exodus 14:14 to find more wisdom for our battle against white noise. How else do we fight the battle according to this verse?

We strap on the armor and He does the work. We still our hearts and turn to Him in prayer, ready to listen to His song of Truth and Saving Grace. We hold the Sword of the Spirit, the Word. We ingest it with the pages open and He fills us with all knowledge and understanding and trust. We stand still with our shield. The junk from the world bounces off it and into nothingness, having no part in this Child of God, Redeemed and Made Holy.

I think I have forever thought that I needed to strap on the armor and go charging forth. It's partly my personality, but I don't think I'm alone either. The idea of strapping on armor makes most of us think we have this huge responsibility to undertake.

Turn to Isaiah 6:4-7. How did Isaiah feel about the matter?

I'm unclean. I can't battle. I'm world-weary. I'm incapable. Isaiah had his own white noise. Even the greatest prophets have white noise, but notice that even all this noise, God will use to point us to Christ.

Our task is to stand and let the coal touch our lips. Our sins are atoned for, our imperfections, our weaknesses are God's greatest glories when we stand ready for His touch.

You need only be silent. You need only be still.

Well, white noise, you just met your worst enemy. I call Him Savior.

Thank you, Lord, for Your great faithfulness, for always, always being ready on our behalf. Calm my troubled spirit when the world reaches in. Refresh my soul with Your Word. Be in every day, every moment, and every heartbeat. In Jesus we pray, Amen.

Exploration

Choose one tool given to us by God as a gift of His grace, that we strap on daily in the Spirit, from the list in Ephesians 6:10-18. How does this tool serve you in your daily life, with your family, in your marriage, with friends, or in your church or your community? Help us see some examples of the Armor of God at work in real life.

Who do you have in your life that helps you to filter out the noise, whether internal or external, and helps you discern Truth from untruth?

he calls me awake

Isaiah 43:4a
Because you are precious in my eyes,
and honored, and I love you…

week seven

He Calls Me Awake

Wake Up to Love
Wake Up, Dark World!
The Night Before Christmas
When Awake Just Isn't Working
Coffee, Tea, and Jesus Please

heart verse

Morning by morning he awakens;
he awakens my ear
to hear as those who are taught.
Isaiah 50:4b

he calls me awake
▼▼▼▼

day one
Wake Up to Love

Who has an alarm song? Do you wake up to an annoying and persistent beep-beep-beep, or a duck quack? Does your alarm blast out one of your favorite tunes in the wee hours of the morning to motivate you to get out of bed? How do you wake up?

My husband sets our alarm every night. It has been his job since we were newlyweds in our tiny studio apartment in St. Louis. I don't remember how he got this job, but every night he would flip a switch on our old-school clock radio, make sure it was tuned to a local rock station, and climb into bed next to me. At 6am our alarm would sound to a roll of the dice, either an alternative grunge rock hit or a loud obnoxious DJ with morning pizazz. You can see why we were really excited when the cell phone alarm transformed our lives and we could pick the song we wanted for our morning wake up call. It's still my husband's job, but now he picks a song, inputs it into the alarm settings and voila – praise music is our jam every morning at 6am.

There are still limits to this set up. Dave picks the song, but at some point one of us inevitably tires of it. "If I have to wake up to So-and-So singing Such-and-Such one more time…" "If I have to hear the Fill-in-the-Band-Name remind me that God thinks I'm special for the fortieth time…" I bet many of you are as friendly to get out of bed in the morning as we are, and even your favorite artists grate on your nerves, simply because it's 6am.

God thinks of mornings a little differently than I do. In God's economy, each day is fresh, not the repetition of a long-ago set alarm. In fact, God, Himself, awakens us each day. He is our Dawn and our Bright Morning Star, bidding us to rise.

Please turn to Isaiah 50:4-7 in your Bible. What does God wake us up for and what does He do when He wakes us up?

This passage, like so many others in Isaiah that we have studied, is a prophecy of The Servant, a prophecy of Jesus. Jesus is the One who is never rebellious, who inclines His ear to the Father's calling, not just once, not when He needed it, but every time. Because of His work for our salvation, we can have a relationship with God where His mercies are new and always available to us. He wakes us every morning, the Father's gentle breath of forgiveness on our face, before we even roll out of bed. He makes us ready for our callings in the wee hours, whether that's at 6am, 11am, 4pm, or 11pm. Just for fun, what time do you usually wake in the morning?

God is right there, and so are His mercies every day your eyes open to a new day (or night for all our third-shift friends). Our passage in Isaiah reminds us that He is the One who Wakes. He sustains our eyes to open, our breath to fill our cells, and our muscles to strengthen us for the day ahead. Scripture tells us that the Father, unlike blaring alarms, is found in the gentle whisper (1 Kings 19:12), but sometimes he'll use trumpet blasts to wake us up to His presence (Acts 16:26). However He chooses to do it, He awakens us.

We awaken because He determined that this day is for His work.

When I take in that first cognizant breath, that's the Spirit, letting me know that God has designed this day for me as His child to go forth. He has plans for me. He's not finished with me yet. And He has planned His work for me.

What is the work of each new day?

"The LORD has given me the tongue of those who are taught that I may know how to sustain with a word him who is weary…" (Isaiah 50:4)

Jesus in us, means that we wake up to love.

We wake up to say, "I am loved."

We wake up to say, "Who needs His love?"

We wake up to reach His Hand into the lives of those who need His fresh breath in their lives.

We wake up to Love.

Christ woke up from the tomb. He did not stay underneath the covers of darkness and sin and shame. He rose up on that bright morning in the garden many years ago, and that bright morning lives in us to reach a weary world each and every day.

Wake up to Love today. Hear what God says in His Word about you and for you. You are valued and treasured. Go and share it with a world that does not know the bright morning Son like we know Him.

Wake up to Love.

Exploration
What is your usual morning routine?

What does the message of "Wake up to Love" speak into your life?

he calls me awake
▼ ▼ ▼ ▼

day two
Wake Up, Dark World!

Do you have to wake anyone up in the morning? Is it one of your tasks to rustle someone from solid sleep to up-and-at-'em? This happens to be part of my morning routine in this stage of life. I get up, exercise, shower, and then begin making my rounds.

Round One – attempted wake up of all people under the age of 15 in the house. Round One is usually successful for 1-2 children, most often my boys and I am convinced this is only because they like breakfast. "Food please, immediately please," is their sleepy-faced morning song.

Rounds Two and Three – these rounds are usually successful for waking one more child. Jyeva is a reluctant waker, but can be dressed and ready within five minutes. She is the sleepyhead shuffling to the restroom, absentmindedly mumbling "Good Morning, Mom" as she closes the door.

Rounds 4, 5, 6, 7, and I-give-up are for my eldest. Mornings are not her strong suit. We used to bring her to school in her pajamas and tell her to get dressed in the van. She would comply, but the next morning was more of the same. Nothing we have ever done has motivated her to rise up from slumber earlier than absolutely necessary and we have been creative!

God gets creative with His people too. Read Isaiah 52:1-8. What wake-up call does God give the people in this passage?

In the space of a few verses, God tries to wake up, to rouse His people with the topics of beautiful garments, circumcision...and feet. While these things might not seem to fit together at first glance, they are all reminders of the covenant promise of our God, a reminder of who they are as Yahweh's people and what they were set apart for — sharing His Name.

God wants His people to arise. The people at the time of Isaiah's writing seemed at the least vaguely unconcerned with what God was doing in their lives and with the people of Israel as a whole. We can find ourselves so entrenched in our own lives, our own struggle, our own busyness that we become content with sitting on the ground in the dust, just like them. Who wants a dusty life when we can have an *awake* one?

What does choosing to sit in the dust look like to you? What examples would you give of modern day unconcern for God and His Kingdom?

Then, before we assume too much, there is another kind of sitting in the dust. We all have times in our life of grief and pain. We can have compassion on those who sit in the dust, and shine light and hope when the road is difficult. Sometimes people experience the reaches of abuse inflicted by another person, and it sends them into the dust. Sometimes people experience the weight of life and bills and decisions that need to be made with few choices in sight. These dust-sitting times of struggle may look different for each of us. Whatever our dust and darkness, though, each of our journeys reflect this common thread...

God awakens our souls to Life in Christ Jesus.

Open your Bible to Psalm 57. Read the entire, life-giving Psalm, if you have a moment, or Psalm 57:7-10 if time is short. What circumstances surround the psalmist's experiences, and for what is the psalmist woken?

What are your circumstances? Where has the devil tempted you to sit in the dust? There have been times when God has let us sit, knowing we need a moment, but in Him, never in the dust. He invites us to truly Live.

You may hear "Awake!" as a command. What I hear is a God desperate to invite you in to the things that really matter.

Psalm 57 and Isaiah 52 fill us with the whole truth. Living looks a whole lot like getting up and going out. Living in Jesus looks like a community called the Church surrounding us and ready to help, if we let it.

Raise your hand if you're tired of being apathetic. Raise your hand if you're ready to go do life. Here is the invitation. The Spirit is in us. God gives us five ways to fight past complacency and ordinary in Isaiah 52:7-8. Choose one that God is calling you to embrace today and circle it:

> *How beautiful upon the mountains*
>   *are the feet of him* **who brings good news,**
> **who publishes peace, who brings good news of happiness,**
>   **who publishes salvation,**
>   **who says to Zion, "Your God reigns."**

Do you see the five? I added bold lettering to help you find them. Let's go through some ways these complacency-fighters may work in our own lives.

We publish peace.
   Maybe this looks like family communication, work communication, or mediating between the grouchy people around us. Maybe this means keeping your children from throwing each other under the bus. Our message of Peace is something a hurting world needs. It looks like grace and forgiveness, instead of false security and broken promises. We can be the voice of Peace in our households, in our workplaces, in our churches and our communities. We can honor one another by assuming the best of others and leaving stereotypes and generalizations at the door.

We bring good news.
   I could use some good news! How about you? This world needs some good news. Good news starts with a little praise and thanksgiving like we see in Psalm 57:9. We can share our thankfulness with God, but we can also share our thankfulness with others and bring some good into their lives. Send a note, share a meme, tell someone they matter.

This good news is often unexpected in people's lives. We share LIFE when we share thanksgiving for and with one another. It is no mistake that we bring "good news of happiness" (Isaiah 52:7). You matter. You matter to me and to God. Can anything make us happier, more filled with life? Happiness isn't everything, but in its purest form, its Jesus-shaped form, it's connected to the Good News of what He has done for us.

We publish salvation.
Someone needs the message of Love. Someone needs specifically the message of Loved Enough to Save. Someone needs the John 3:16 kind of Love. We have so many realms we can "publish" in – face-to-face, over the phone, text messaging, on social media. Publish the message, friends.

You are loved enough to Save.

We sing for joy.
You cannot stay asleep while singing. I'm pretty sure it's a proven fact. One of my favorite ways to awaken my kids is by singing the song "Good Morning" from *Singin' in the Rain*. A good show tune is always sure to arouse. They may grumble, but I know they secretly love it. We can let the joy come out in our homes and in our lives. Some days it will be more obvious and forth coming than others, but just let it out. Rise and Shine and Give God the Glory, literally. His Joy is always knocking around in that soul of yours somewhere. He promises it as a gift unchanging. Let it out when it rises up.

We offer comfort.
I think this goes back to a world sitting in the dust.

How can we begin to help? Who around you is desolate and hurting? As God tends to our own souls and we publish how that tending has changed everything that was black and grey and dusty into beauty and color, someone else's ears may be awakened by the Word we publish, through the Spirit, and what they hear is Life. There is no better Comfort than a compassionate heart sharing God's Word of Truth and Love.

Morning may not be your jam, but Life certainly is. You were made for it. You were picked up from the dust by His Salvation, His Love. Now it's time to publish it. Don't waste a day, don't listen to the devil's schemes of tuning out what matters for what is momentary.

We are awake and truly alive in Christ.

Exploration
Who has the hardest time getting out of bed in your house and what does that look like for you?

Which one of the 5 exhortations from Isaiah do you feel calling to you today – comfort, publish, peace, sing, or bring good news, and why?

What creative ways have you tried to awaken yourself or others spiritually, with the Spirit's help?

he calls me awake
▼ ▼ ▼

day three
The Night Before Christmas

There seem to be two types of music people in this world and I do not mean rock-n-roll versus classical. There's the *it's-99-days-until-Christmas!* kind of person or the *wait-until-Thanksgiving-please* kind of person. Which one are you? Do you rock to the Christmas tunes with abandon in mid-July or do you avoid the home and garden section of Walmart and Target in October because instead of fall foliage and ferns, you feel stressed as they push the fake evergreens and strands of twinkly lights out onto the floor?

Ok, that's not fair. There is a whole spectrum between those two ends for our Christmas music choices. What are your preferences for Christmas music and when and where it's played?

How often do we think there is one right way in any given situation? Let's remind ourselves of a familiar passage in Isaiah 9:2, 6-7 and hear it in an outside-the-box different. Today, it's time for an advent devotion, no matter what time of year it is for you. Write your own paraphrase of the message you find in Isaiah 9:2,6-7 below:

God gives the Israelites the promise of Christmas, a few hundred years early. I'm convinced one purpose in this is so that they can muscle through the dark season to come. In Isaiah 9, God, through the prophet, is prepping the Israelites to live in 400 years of silence before the coming of the Baby, Jesus. During these 400 years there will be no new prophets and no new words from God. I'm not sure we can imagine a time like this. We are New Testament believers with the full Word of God in our hands when we hold the Bible. God hadn't yet given the Word in its fullness to His people. We do know darkness, but we do not know the darkness of a silent God.

One night, a long time ago in Bethlehem town, a child was born to us. The Word made flesh dwelt among us. The temple curtain was torn. His canon of the Word was completed for us. We no longer live in silence. We have daily Hope in a Living Spirit that chooses us as His dwelling place.

The message of this hope can so easily be lost in the banter of our beliefs about the right and proper time to put out decorations, the correct greeting, the proper placement of the wise men in the nativity, and the social media opinions that attempt to drown out the other side.

We love to be right — so much so that we sometimes sacrifice the meaning and its message. That's one reason to contemplate the hope of Isaiah's words outside of the calendar Christmas season. When we do, we can focus in from a different vantage point.

The message of Christmas is the message of a God who is awake. There was a night before Christmas, a dark night, a *silent* night…

and then the world awakened to a Baby Boy.

There were a few thousand nights before Christmas when people were waiting and hoping and praying, and all along God had a plan. Silence wasn't something that sounded wonderful in the way we dream it up with our candlelight services on Christmas Eve. Yet, God was awake and listening to the cries of His people. He plotted the proper time. He chose just the right moment, and one morning, Hope was born.

>The angels awakened in the skies…

>The wise men awakened from their study, to find sure and solid Truth…

>The weary world wakes up Christmas morning to find that everlasting Joy has dawned…

Isaiah doesn't stop there. Look at Isaiah 9:6 again. Because God is awake and hears our cry, He invites us to —

Awaken to Mighty

Awaken to Wonderful

Awaken to Everlasting

Awaken to Peace

Where do you need God's mighty help in your life? Where do you need a touch of wonderful counsel and care? Where do you need to know that this is not all there is, this world, that something is Everlasting? Where do you need some heaven-sent Peace? Write some notes beside each *Awaken to* message above. What do you need from God, what is your prayer at this time and place in your life?

Christ Jesus, born innocent and precious and tiny, has more power in His itty-bitty right pinky finger than we can imagine, but He deigns to bring hope to me, to my family, to my friends, to my church, to my world.

That night before Christmas was so dark, and some seasons in our lives are dark as well. These seasons can feel like God is silent in our own lives. We begin to feel desperate just to get to the time when morning dawns, but God is awake through all of it. He hears. He hears, and never, never will we have to live without Jesus.

So whether it's December or May, let's live with thankfulness in our hearts and on our lips, in the full knowledge that we have a God of Hope, a God who is Awake. Let's share this message with someone who needs it —

Wonderful Counselor
Mighty God
Everlasting Father
Prince of Peace

Our God is Awake.

Exploration
How do you think the message of a God that is awake and not silent can impact the hurting world, the complacent world, or the sin-sick world?

Share which title speaks to you in a particular way today – Our God is...a Wonderful Counselor... a Mighty God... an Everlasting Father... a Prince of Peace... How and why?

he calls me awake
▼ ▼ ▼ ▼

day four
When Awake Just Isn't Working

Ever had a day when you'd like to just go back upstairs, put on your pajamas, crawl back into bed, and hide from the world around you? Yes? This was my day last Tuesday. It took everything I had to leave my clothes on and walk around out where the people live.

These are the kind of days that we are reminded of a hard truth – we are sinners, living in a sinful world. Life isn't always sunshine and roses, but it certainly is worthwhile. As much as I want to slip on my pajamas and hide under my covers, He calls me out for more.

Israel in the Old Testament had plenty of pajama-and-under-the-covers kind of days. Some of these days were their own fault. They chased other gods, let lust have its way, and set aside the opportunities to worship for whatever seemed good at the moment. Sin creeps into our lives in ways we least expect as well. What kinds of personal sins do you think cause under-the-cover days?

We think we're pretty good people; we go to church, we do all right. The Truth is that not one of us is without sin. We have blunt and obvious sin — hurtful words and anger, ignoring our neighbor, the chitter chatter of gossip, and more. We also have the secret sins — hate in our heart, lust, discontentment, thinking more highly of ourselves than we ought.

Please read Isaiah 26:16-19. God leaves hope where we leave sin. What gifts did God give Israel when they turned to Him *in* their sin?

As we read, we hear the Israelites proclaim their allegiance to the Lord and the Lord alone. They recognize their sin and the mess they've made. They also look around and see the sin and mess of the nations around them. What sin and mess do other people often bring into our lives that cause under-the-cover days for us?

In Isaiah 26, the people of Israel see the mess, but in this instance, they also recognize the goodness and necessity of the Lord's discipline. Consequences happen, but instead of sneaking away, they cling tightly to the promise that only the resurrection can offer –eternal life and the perspective that comes with it.

Sometimes God not only gives me grace, He also gives me excessively practical advice for these exact situations in my own life. Isn't it nice when it works out like that? What can we learn for life from Isaiah 26?

First, they pray:
   …they poured out whispered prayer… (Isaiah 26:16)

He wants to hear our sin. Sometimes we think, "He knows it, why should we say it?" Why confess it aloud?

Hearing it from our lips, poured out from our hearts, gives Him the opportunity to pour mercy into us.

He pours into us forgiveness and life. He pours tenderness and healing. Do you have past sins that sit on your heart like a boulder? Do you ever feel like if people found out your real story, they would never look at you the same way again? God says, "No. I heal. I restore." He will take that sin with our confession, forgive it, and use it for His testimony. He has a plan.

What wisdom can you find in 1 Thessalonians 5:17?

Pray unceasingly also means pray about all of it, even the ugly stuff. God invites us to pour out every last sin and temptation to Him.

Pour it out to Him, and watch Him pour in.

Then, they rise:
   Your dead shall live; their bodies shall rise.
      You who dwell in the dust, awake and sing for joy!
               (Isaiah 26:19a)

God invites us to confess, not to make us sit in the dust, but to pick us up out of our shame and pour Himself into us.

What does Psalm 23:5 tell us about God?
This exchange of pouring out my sin and Him pouring in forgiveness is part of the Overflowing Cup of Who He is. He fills with mercy. He fills with grace, and He fills some more, releasing us from the burden of our own incapabilities and inadequacies. "Let me take that," He says, "I already carried that cross." He gives us His life-giving Spirit instead of sin and shame.

When faced with our sin, we can look to Jesus, or we can look away. We can crawl back into our jammies and hide under the covers, or we can let Him give us a New Day.

Pour it out to Him. He pours in.

Our cup overflows with mercy and grace. Our shame is gone! I pray you know this Truth in your life today…there is forgiveness and grace, poured on you for every last sin, every last fail, for pajama days and rockstar days and every day in between.

He is our Overflowing Cup.

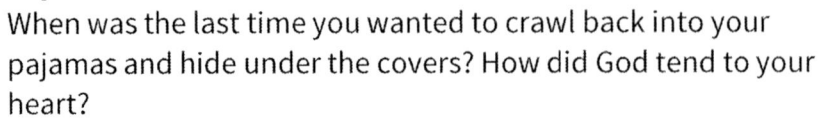

Exploration
When was the last time you wanted to crawl back into your pajamas and hide under the covers? How did God tend to your heart?

Read John 17:1-5 and identify the following:
Who is praying and why?

What does he identify as eternal life and how does this perspective change each of our days?

he calls me awake
▼ ▼ ▼ ▼

day five
Coffee, Tea, and Jesus Please

How do you feel about coffee? I tend toward ardent fan. I'm totally on the bandwagon for the coffee graphics that proclaim its wonderfulness.

"Come here, you big beautiful cup of coffee and lie to me about all we're going to get done today."

"All this girl needs today is a little bit of coffee and a whole lot of Jesus."

"First I drink the coffee, then I do the things."

Perhaps you are more Captain Picard, and a little less Captain Janeway. Is tea your bag? What gets you going in the morning? What ignites your energy for the day? What wakes you up — literally or figuratively?

God tells us that we all need something to wake us up. We all were once sleeping through life, but He had a better plan, a better way.

Metaphorically, the Bible talks about sin as our sleep drug. What does Proverbs 6:4-11 teach us about sleep?

We all know sleep isn't a terrible thing, in fact we need it. So, what's the biggest concept in Proverbs here? Sin can make us metaphorically sleepy. It closes our eyes to what is right and good. It's surprisingly cozy and comfortable, lulling us into a complacency that leads to more sin. We love comfort so much that the light around us dims and we don't even notice until we are standing in utter darkness.

Sometimes sin jumps on us when we are tired, quite literally! For example, we might disrespect our husbands or lash out at our families when we haven't had enough sleep or are waning from a long day. We feel better for an instant, but then the darkness comes.

Complacency can creep in when we skip church or avoid our Bible study group over and over again, for other things that sound fun or for the busyness of life. It feels good for a second to sleep in or not have to chit chat, but then the darkness comes.

We fall asleep in sin when we have a juicy conversation with friends at work. It feels good to talk about someone else and know that your own shame is not the topic of the meaty conversation. It can't hurt her if she doesn't know, right? Then the darkness comes in.

Sin doesn't wear a bright sign that says "Beware!" Instead, it wraps us up slowly like a cozy blanket and then attempts to strangle us at the last minute, when we're all tucked in.

Ephesians 5:6-14 is one of my favorite passages of Scripture and it's about being awake. It is practical and bears the truth of the relationship between light, darkness, sleeping, and being an Awake Child of God. Read Ephesians 5:6-14 below and circle or underline any reference you find that speaks of dark, light, sleeping, or awake:

> *Let no one deceive you with empty words, for because of these things the wrath of God comes upon the sons of disobedience. Therefore do not become partners with them; for at one time you were darkness, but now you are light in the Lord. Walk as children of light (for the fruit of light is found in all that is good and right and true), and try to discern what is pleasing to the Lord. Take no part in the unfruitful works of darkness, but instead expose them. For it is shameful even to speak of the things that they do in secret. But when anything is exposed by the light, it becomes visible, for anything that becomes visible is light. Therefore it says,*
> >   *"Awake, O sleeper,*
> >   *and arise from the dead,*
> >   *and Christ will shine on you."*

At one time you were darkness means we are no longer darkness! Can you hear the grace? We are now light in the Lord Jesus. That means we are Daytime and Sunlight. We are not third shift, 3am, sluggish and sleepy children of God, trapped in sin. We are *Awake*.

How do you wake up in the middle of a gossip session, especially when it feels so good? How do you wake up when the words of disrespect pour out of your mouth? Ephesians gives insight for these questions.

Do not become partners. (Ephesians 5:7)
Some people were meant to be avoided like the plague. This is not you being hurtful or failing to eat with tax collectors. This is you knowing your own limit. This is caring for others but knowing when you aren't at the place to resist the temptation. Love every neighbor, but don't make your closest friends those who partner with darkness.

Do not speak of shameful things. (Ephesians 5:12)
I know it's the worst when everyone else knows what happened in the royal marriage that was shameful and catastrophic and you don't. (Sorry royals, I know you have kept the marriages pretty stellar as of late.) If it's someone else's shame, it's not our business to speak of. This goes for the divorce of the couple next door, or the mental illness that befalls someone's child. If it's not our story, it's not our story to share. We can care, and love, and support, but there is a fine line between passing along prayers and passing along a story that is incomplete and not our own.

Let Christ Shine.
Bright Morning Star is His name. When we let go of what we want, the light of His glory is so bright that we can't help but live *Awake*. Let the Spirit out, my friends! Let Him out. Tea and coffee, even a triple shot mocha double skinny dark has nothing on a real and living God inside of us. We can pray — *Lord shine through me. Let my life shine of only You and always You.*

Write Ephesians 5:16 below to end with a good reminder that you are Awake in Christ —

Our time on this earth is so short. I want to live Awake. I *am* Awake in Him. Why would I want to go back to that darkness, even for a brief stroll? No, thank you. Grab your giant mug, inhale the scent of forgiveness, take a moment in prayer, and let Christ Shine.

Exploration

What do you do in when gossip or disrespect from your own mouth seems imminent? Do you have a way to tamp it down and let Light out instead?

How can you let Christ shine today?

he calls me gathered

Isaiah 43:4a
Because you are precious in my eyes,
and honored, and I love you…

week eight
He Calls Me Gathered

No Longer a Foreigner to Grace
Worship is Life
I Love My Shepherd
Promises to Keep
Gathered to Go

heart verse

He will raise a signal for the nations
and will assemble the banished of Israel,
and gather the dispersed of Judah
from the four corners of the earth.
Isaiah 11:12

he calls me gathered
▼ ▼ ▼

day one
No Longer a Foreigner to Grace

The day we moved to Haiti was exciting and exhilarating. We got up at 3am, headed to the Detroit airport with our giant suitcases, hugged our selfless middle-of-the-night chauffeur friends and headed off for adventure.

My first thought when we arrived in Haiti was, "We can handle this!" With the warm greetings of our Haitian friends, our bellies full with plantain and celebratory cake, and the distraction of unpacking and settling in, the culture around me seemed a curiosity, rather than shocking.

It took little more than four days and a trip to the Haitian marketplace to feel thrown completely off my footing, to know that "we can handle this" was hopeful at best, a serious delusion at worst.

In the marketplace, there were people everywhere, and I mean everywhere. I have shopped foreign marketplaces before. I've traveled all over. I don't love bartering, but I have some skills. I enjoy people, crazy mixes of smells, and the sound of vibrant language overlapping in the pleasant chaos of the day's busyness. But I have never had to do it for my survival. I wasn't there just to browse and procure a few souvenirs for friends back home. I needed groceries, and I needed them on a limited missionary budget. I needed to figure out how to cook said groceries, and I needed to not get hit by a mototaxi trying to lug them home.

I stood in the marketplace that morning and realized I was a foreigner. I was an outsider. I had no clue what I was doing, and do you know what that translates to? It translates to that feeling of utterly alone. Standing in the middle of the crowded marketplace, the sounds dissipated around me, the tears welled up and I realized, in the end, that it's just me on this very literal island. No one here knows me, really knows me. If I fell, would someone pick me up? If I disappeared, would anyone notice?

In the marketplace, lost in my lonely thoughts, I felt a tug on my elbow that brought me back to the movement and the noises all around me. I looked into the chocolate eyes of my friend Sydney, who placed her hand on my arm, held on to it with a lock-tight grip, and said, "Heidi, I am here."

That day in the market, Sydney gathered me. She didn't just gather me to reassure me and keep me safe. She also gathered me to be a part of her people. Our friends in Haiti did absolutely everything they could each day to make us part of their lives. To welcome us, yes, but also to gather us as part of the family of God, a community no language divides.

Have you ever been the foreigner? Alone in another country, another town, another family? Think past the obvious. Have you ever been left standing in the high school cafeteria looking for a place to sit? Have you ever had to walk into a new church praying it felt like home? Have you ever rolled over in bed and realized afresh that the other side now lies empty and this world of loss is something harder than you ever imagined? What have been your experiences with aloneness, whether in travel, loss, life in school, work, anywhere really?

God promises that in all of our aloneness, all of our wanderings, all of our cast-aside and walked-away and went-far-off, He will gather us to Himself.

Isaiah records this promise in Isaiah 56:5-8. What does God say about those who are far off in these verses?

Child, you are better than a son, better than a daughter. That means that you who were once a stranger to God, a foreigner to grace and mercy, are now more than family.

You are gathered.

He has joined you to Himself, gathered you up from your dark places or your regular middle-of-the-road day and brought you into relationship with Him.

Isaiah 56:7 proclaims that He brings us to His Holy Mountain and makes us joyful in His house of prayer. God made someone else joyful in His house of prayer. She also felt like an outsider, a less than, and wondered if she was foreign to God in her barrenness. Look at Hannah's story fresh. Read 1 Samuel 1:10-16. What various clues can you find that speak of the struggle in Hannah's life?

Hannah brought all of her anxiety, all of her burden, all of her pain before the true God. Her heart overflowed, "pouring out her soul" before the Lord. If you think that Hannah's prayer was polite, I would offer up a different vantage point. The Bible specifically identifies for us in 1 Samuel 1:10 that she was speaking with the Lord in great anxiety and vexation. Various English definitions of vexation include annoyance, exasperation, indignation, and aggravation. The Hebrew word for *in distress,* which we find the ESV translation of 1 Samuel 1:10 is *marat*[ix], or *bitter, bitterness*. Hannah didn't just pour out her requests, she poured out her bitterness in this house of prayer.

Hannah was gathered by the Lord.

He gathered her up to hear her bitterness, hear her dissension, to hear her shock and her distress at a world that was not fair. Is it possible that Hannah wondered in her distress if she even knew the Lord? Did Her beloved Savior feel foreign to her in her struggle? Have you ever been there?

You are gathered.

This is how God gathers. Maybe the house of prayer is simply honest relationship with God. Peak back at Isaiah 56. What did the Lord want from His people? He just wanted them to come to

Him. Look for the following phrases in Isaiah 56 and note the verse reference where you find it next to the phrase —

...To love the name of the Lord...
...to minister to Him...
...to hold fast...
...to place our sacrifices, on His altar...

You are gathered and He promises to gather others as well. That means all the Hannahs you have around you, bitter and struggling with something — He is gathering them. When He brings you to Himself, whether in bitterness or joy, He will use you to gather and gather and gather some more.

You are gathered. You may look a foreigner in this present land. You may feel a foreigner in your family, your church, or your culture. You may have some annoyance, some frustrations, or some distrust stored up to pour out before Him.

Go ahead and do it.

You are no longer a foreigner to His grace. You are gathered.

Trust in the One who holds you tight.

Exploration
Present your requests before the Lord. Set a timer and challenge yourself to pray for 10 minutes straight, with no distractions. Please feel free to pray longer, but let's challenge each other to pour the cares of the day out to Him and spend time with Him, and Him alone, for just a bit. If you'd like to share some prayer requests, please feel free to do so in the margins of your pages.

he calls me gathered

▼ ▼ ▼ ▼

day two
Worship is Life

Ever feel like you need a flashing neon sign from God? I think we all have at one time or another asked God to show us something clearly. Most of the time, God doesn't really work like that — neon signs and flashing lights — but today we get a treat.

Please open your Bible to Isaiah 11 and read just one verse, Isaiah 11:12. Copy that verse into the space below to really help it stick in our brain.

If we needed that flashing neon sign from God, here it is. God raises a signal and holds it high for all people to see, crying out with arms outstretched —

"Come to Me. Let Me gather."

We look for giant billboards and signs from God, telling us what to do and where to go, but the signal is no mystery. The signal is very simply Christ Jesus saying, "Come."

God makes this clear over and over again throughout the Scriptures, but Isaiah 11 is like a giant beacon, shining light into the darkness of the unknown. Back up and read Isaiah 11:1-5. What connections to Jesus can you find in these verses?

Don't these verses just make you want to worship Him? This is no mistake. Jesus is the signal, raised high for us to gather around, but how will the world know?

What if God uses our worship as the bull horn of salvation for the people? And the billboard of encouragement and discernment for one another?

What is worship? His Word going out, His promises proclaimed, and His people responding. The Word surely does the work, but what do people see when they look around them and see worship?

They see Life in Worship and worship as the way we live our life.

Worship is a gift! Worship may at times be just between you and God, but mostly, it was meant to be communal. It was meant to be you, God, and God's people. It speaks life back and forth between the followers of Christ a s they share His Word with one another, and it speaks to those on the outside looking in as well.

We don't worship for a show. We aren't performers or puppeteers putting on a nice pretty picture for the world around us, but when the people of God gather, Life flows. Forgiveness flows. Confession happens. Mercy is given. Truth is spoken. Love is bestowed. Grace rains down. Encouragement builds.

God gathers His people. Only by His grace do we get out of bed on Sunday morning or Thursday night or whenever else, to worship alongside family, friends, and strangers. Only by His grace do we remember to pick up the family devotion book off the table and share His Peace with one another. Only by His grace will we be brought together in the heavens to sing with all the saints and angels, *"Holy, holy, holy, is the Lord God Almighty, who was and is and is to come!"* (Revelation 4:8)

Jesus is always concerned with reaching the nations around us, the people around us. He reaches out and sweeps in the people with His ever-loving arms. He comes to us.

Listen to what will happen. The Signal that is Christ Jesus will come again and the worship that results will be like nothing the world has ever seen. Indeed, every nation will see and hear. Write out Philippians 2:10 below to see this Truth on the page.

Worship is Life and it speaks Life to a hurting world.

Worship with your life, friends. Worship for the Life He has given you and let Life flow to others by the act of your worship. Watch Him gather!

Lord, we worship You. We adore You. You alone are faithful, Lord. You alone are worthy. Let our worship be in honesty and in Truth. Let it be only for You. May You use each of us as Your signals, as Your people proclaiming Your Honor to all the earth. In Jesus we pray, Father, through Your everlasting Spirit. Amen!

Exploration

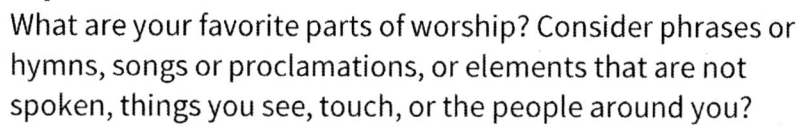

What are your favorite parts of worship? Consider phrases or hymns, songs or proclamations, or elements that are not spoken, things you see, touch, or the people around you?

What is special the people and the place where you worship weekly? What makes your church and church family unique?

Bonus: Look at Isaiah 11:1-12 in full. What promises do you find? What will gathering look like when Jesus comes back for us?

he calls me gathered

▼ ▼ ▼ ▼

day three
I Love My Shepherd

I like blankets.

When I was little they were my comfort, with their fuzzy middles and their silky edges. They wrapped me up when I needed to feel safe and warmed my toes and arms on winter nights. My mom knew that when I was sad, I needed a hug and my hole-y blue blanket, raged and worn, full of holes, so I could love it to literal pieces.

What speaks comfort into your life?

What physical manifestations of God's warmth and goodness has He blessed you with in this life?

God encourages us to fix our eyes on the eternal, but He leaves us with the temporal as a bonus, small reminders that He is good. He is our truest comfort on cold days and in the dark of night.

Throughout Scripture, God gives us a vision of comfort in the metaphor of the Good Shepherd. This Good Shepherd consistently gathers His sheep. Open to Isaiah 40:10-11. Which words or phrases found there are most comforting to you today?

God is a mighty God, but here we see and hear His tenderness as well. God is so fantastically perfect that He is complete in a way which we cannot fathom. Our mighty God, our powerful Good Shepherd goes out to defeat the wolves of this world, to defeat the devil who tries to destroy us, but He also holds you in His arms. He gathers every part of you to Him and will never let you go. He gathers His people to His chest and loves, loves, loves, and loves some more.

Without even knowing it, I named my blog after Psalm 23. Sometimes the Holy Spirit brings the Word to mind and we figure it out later.

How familiar are you with Psalm 23? List anything that comes to mind about it without looking. If you can't think of anything, don't worry. Today this Psalm will be our focus.

Let's read it together today. Read through Psalm 23, below, slowly. Circle verbs or actions words that ascribe the activities of this mighty, loving Savior:

> The Lord is my shepherd; I shall not want.
>   He makes me lie down in green pastures.
> He leads me beside still waters.
>   He restores my soul.
> He leads me in paths of righteousness
>   for his name's sake.
> Even though I walk through the valley of the shadow of death,
>   I will fear no evil,
> for you are with me;
>   your rod and your staff,
>   they comfort me.
> You prepare a table before me
>   in the presence of my enemies;
> you anoint my head with oil;
>   my cup overflows.
> Surely goodness and mercy shall follow me
>   all the days of my life,
> and I shall dwell in the house of the Lord
>   forever.

He restores. He overflows. He walks with me. He pursues me with mercy. He provides for me. He gathers me around the table and He eats with me.

Let's widen it a bit. Let's think about gather in its fullest sense.

He restores *us*.

He overflows into *us*.

He walks with *us*.

He pursues *us*.

He provides for *us*.

He gathers *us* around the table. He eats with *us*.

We were made for gathering. We were born into a flock. We experience the fullness of Him within the gathering of His people.

I Love My Shepherd is about We Love Our Shepherd...stretching my heart for Christ, and for His people. We are the comfort, dear friends, for our husbands, and those in our homes, in our churches, in our neighborhoods, and in our lives. We speak Jesus into one another's life in a way we wouldn't experience walking this earth on our own.

Let's pray Psalm 23 today for our own needs, but also for one another. Let's thank our Shepherd for just being Himself in all His wonderfulness as well as giving us this life to live together.

Let's do a project together. For exploration today, reread Psalm 23 through three times. (There is space at the end of today's study to work through this activity.)

First – read the Psalm and focus on who God is, as our Shepherd. When you read the Psalm, jot down what you learn about Him.

Spend time in prayer proclaiming His character, such as Provider, Comforter, Leader, etc.

Next – read the Psalm a second time and focus on what Christ the Good Shepherd does for you as an individual. How has he brought His work proclaimed in Psalm 23 to bear in your real life? Where have you seen Him shepherd? Where have you seen Him lead? Through what do you need Him to walk with you?

Last – as you read the Psalm a final time, simply pray over everything that comes to find. Focus on what our Good Shepherd does for His people or for other people in your life. Pray the psalm over anyone in need or ask for God's provision, comfort, and overflow into individuals in your life and/or your church.

We are gathered. We are the sheep of our Shepherd, as well as sheep of the sheepfold. We are loved, cared for, mightily rescued, guided, and filled to the brim with overflowing.

I love my Shepherd. And I know you do, too.

Exploration

Share some of your prayer insights from Psalm 23 with us, fill in the requests you feel comfortable sharing for each prayer round or share some that stick out to you overall.

Round 1 - Who God is as our Shepherd…

Round 2 - What God does for you, as an individual…

Round 3 - What God does for His people, or the people in your life…

he calls me gathered
▼ ▼ ▼

day four
Promises to Keep

My children are promise trackers. If you tell them that we "might" go to visit a friend, it's as good as complete to them. If you suggest there "may be" dessert in the cupboard, you better have checked the status of the cookie package before throwing haphazard statements around.

Children misunderstand the difference between promises and basic conversation. They tend to believe that something stated as a possibility is as sure and certain as the sun rising each day. Adults should be cautious about making promises they can't keep, but it's also an important skill for children to learn that promises are meant for big things, not cookies in the pantry. Life happens, and forgiveness is necessary more often than we'd like.

God makes promises to us in the book of Isaiah, over and over again. These are not maybe-there-will-be-cookies promises. These are big promises. Can you think of any promises you've discovered in the last eight weeks of our study?

God tells us clearly in Isaiah that not one thing is missing, not one promise is left out or abandoned.

Not one promise from God is broken.

> *The virgin shall conceive and bear a son, and shall call His name Immanuel… (Isaiah 7:14)*
>
> *But He was pierced for our transgressions…(Isaiah 53:5)*
>
> *With righteousness He shall judge the poor… (Isaiah 11:4)*
>
> *My Servant shall be exalted... (Isaiah 52:13)*

Hear the truth about God's promises for yourself by reading Isaiah 34:14-16:

> *And wild animals shall meet with hyenas;*
>   *the wild goat shall cry to his fellow;*
> *indeed, there the night bird settles*
>   *and finds for herself a resting place.*
> *There the owl nests and lays*
>   *and hatches and gathers her young in her shadow;*
> *indeed, there the hawks are gathered,*
>   *each one with her mate.*
> *Seek and read from the book of the Lord:*
>   *Not one of these shall be missing;*
>   *none shall be without her mate.*
> *For the mouth of the Lord has commanded,*
>   *and his Spirit has gathered them.*

While goats and fellows, owls and nests in this passage may seem obscure, they couple up. This is also how God's promises work. Isaiah 34:16 brings the obscurity together, reminding us that as we seek and read, our eyes are opened and every promise meets its rightful destination — fulfillment in Christ Jesus.

God does indeed keep His promises and we can see this as He gathers inside the Word itself.

He gathers prophecies up in His Word and fulfills them, like puzzle pieces clicking together over the course of time. This match here and that match there. We are given the privilege of studying them, finding a promise, seeking its fulfillment in the Word and lifting the pieces up in praise to His name.

We may as parents misspeak. Life may happen and promises might fall by the wayside, but God is completely in control. Not one promise falls from His hands. He reigns over the universe, so life doesn't get in the way for Him. He is perfect. He is ever-present. He sees the whole of eternity before Him and He plans accordingly.

How often, however, are we like children and try to hold God to promises He never made? How often do we claim He promised worldly treasures, when He really promised just what we need? How often do we rail at Him for our suffering, when He only promised to be there with us in it? He never guaranteed to give us a life called perfect by our own standards. How often do we demand control in life, when He promised to lead rather than leave us in the white-knuckle life of fear, fighting for control?

God's message in Isaiah through the gathering of prophecy and fulfillment is this —

He gathers up His promises and holds them tightly for just the proper time. Every Word will be fulfilled. When we can't see what He's doing, we lean into His promises that never change.

Not one promise broken...not one.

Because He gathers.

Exploration
What kind of plans disappoint children when they are broken? What kind of plans disappoint us, as adults, when they are broken?

How do you differentiate between a plan that is able to be shifted and a promise that cannot be broken?

What promises of God do you cling to?

he calls me gathered
▼ ▼ ▼ ▼

day five
Gathered to Go

Eight weeks of study, friends. Eight weeks of walking in Truth -
   He Calls You Beloved
   He Calls You Ransomed
   He Calls You Child
   He Calls You Redeemed
   He Calls You Clay
   He Calls You Sought Out
   He Calls You Awake
   He Calls You Gathered

We have stood in the promise that He aggressively pursues us. He picks us up from the dust and lifts our beautiful heads. He infiltrates our lives with restoration and gives salvation to every little piece of brokenness He finds.

Oh, the Truth of it! There is so much joy in a God who loves us enough to proclaim a place for us at His table, a God who chases, a God who brings back, a God who says "Come to Me."

On this last day of study, let's turn to the final chapter of Isaiah's writing. I think you'll find that God's concluding message in this beautiful book is this...

We are gathered to go.

Read Isaiah 66:18-23. What messages of gathering can you find in this passage?

What messages of going can you find in Isaiah 66:18-23?

The message is not just that God gathers us, but He gathers us *to gather those around us*. He reaches His arm out and sweeps up not just me and you, but all of those we love, our offspring, and our neighbors, and our communities by the simple act of being available to be gathered, rather than closing our hearts off from knowing people more and sharing Jesus deeply.

The message of Isaiah from beginning to end is consistently – people matter to God.

He will do anything to reach His people. He will send us to the coastlands (Isaiah 66:19). He will have us go and fetch the brothers (Isaiah 66:20). He'll use planes, trains, automobiles, camels, sheep, mustard seeds, pastors, teachers, and any other person, place, or thing to get to His people (Isaiah 66:20). Day by day, He is faithful to gather. From workday to rest, He is available and ready and willing to meet with us and seek with us. He will not desert us now.

He teaches us to go.

Go...
  ...because He uses any means necessary to get to us.

Go...
  ...and use any means necessary to get to Him. Join and lead. Gather for Bible study and for worship, start and maintain relationships, allow more time for conversation.

Go...
  ...and use any means necessary to reach the world. Remember, our primary means, the greatest of these means are Faith, Hope, and Love centered in Christ Jesus, our Redeemer.

Go...
  ...let all flesh, every heart, know what you know — Tell them that in Jesus, they are called Loved, they are called Ransomed, they are called Sought Out.

Go...
  ...loved, honored, encouraged, held, and entrusted.

Go...
  ...worshiping, giving glory, lifting high, offering up the good, the hard, and the daily.

I wonder what message of Isaiah sticks with you the most? Which one is stickiest in this season of your life? Circle the title below that reminds you that He declares you worthy in Christ.

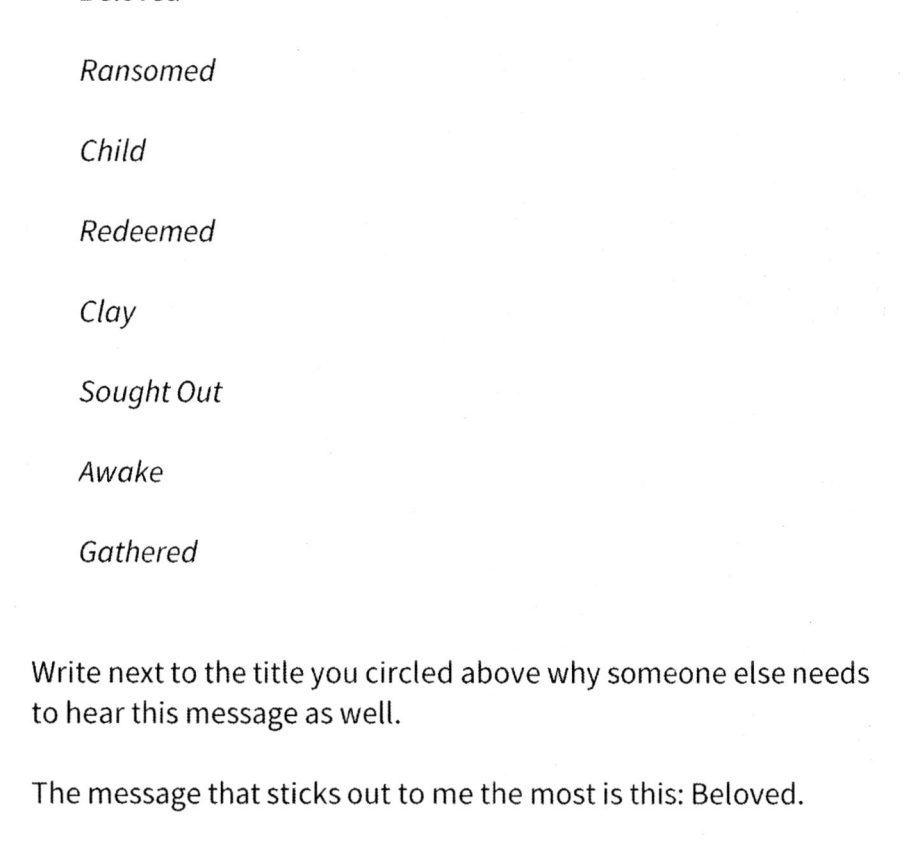

Beloved

Ransomed

Child

Redeemed

Clay

Sought Out

Awake

Gathered

Write next to the title you circled above why someone else needs to hear this message as well.

The message that sticks out to me the most is this: Beloved.

I am loved.

You are loved.

God says it plainly, for all the world to see, in Isaiah 43:4 –

*Because you are precious in my eyes,
   and honored, and I love you...*

What woman has never heard that they are loved...with a love that never gives up, that never quits, and never lets go? Share one woman that comes to mind in your own life.

And so, we go.

I'd rather be a part of the gathering. Because when I look around me, it breaks my heart to know that even one woman, one young girl, one precious child of God would cross my path without knowing the message that I know:

He Calls Me Loved.

Go Loved. Give Love.

He calls you Loved.

Exploration
Who in your life do you gather, with the message of God's love?

Let's do this. Let's gather. Who can you gather with? Who can you tell? Whether in person, with an individual or group, on social media, share one message from our study today. Use the hashtags #ilovemyshepherd and #hecallsmeloved or tag us on social media so we can gather alongside you and share the message that He calls us loved together.

he calls me loved

References

[i] Engelbrecht, Edward A., general ed., *The Lutheran Study Bible* [ESV], (St. Louis: Concordia Publishing House), 2009, 1084-1087.

[ii] "Bible Hub Interlinear Bible." http://biblehub.com/hebrew/4131.htm, accessed January 29, 2018

[iii] Henry, Matthew. "Isaiah." *Matthew Henry's Concise Commentary.* https://www.biblegateway.com/resources/matthew-henry/Isaiah, accessed July 1, 2018.

[iv] Engelbrecht, Edward A., general ed., *The Lutheran Study Bible* [ESV], (St. Louis: Concordia Publishing House), 2009, 6 and 210

[v] Engelbrecht, Edward A., general ed., *The Lutheran Study Bible* [ESV], (St. Louis: Concordia Publishing House), 2009, 1086.

[vi] "Bible Hub Interlinear Bible." http://biblehub.com/greek/5008.htm, accessed February 12, 2018

[vii] "Bible Hub Interlinear Bible." http://biblehub.com/hebrew/1350.htm, accessed June 30, 2018.

[viii] "The Church's One Foundation." http://www.hymnary.org/hymn/LSB2006/644, accessed February 12, 2018.

[ix] "Bible Hub Interlinear Bible." http://biblehub.com/hebrew/4751.htm, accessed February 13, 2018.

Thank you for studying with me! If you have any thoughts, questions, or would like permission to copy a portion of this book, please contact the author, Deaconess Heidi Goehmann, LCSW, LIMHP at ilovemyshepherd.com@gmail.com. I would love to hear from you! You can also follow I Love My Shepherd on Facebook, Instagram, and Twitter. Find complimentary videos and podcasts to accompany this study on the I Love My Shepherd YouTube channel and I Love My Shepherd: The Podcast, wherever you get your podcasts. You can always find me, as well as articles and resources for mental health, genuine community, and life together at ilovemyshepherd.com

I am indebted to my family who loves me every day whether I cook them dinner or call out for pizza while I tend to my computer screen and write. I could not do this work without the love and support and cheerleading of Dave, Macee, Jonah, Jyeva, and Zeke, as well as my Coffeehouse Girls, Sarah, and my sisters. A huge thank you to my awesome readers who pick up an I Love My Shepherd resource and then go breath hope into a world in need, rather than let the Word sit on a shelf. We spur one another on in this beautiful life together and for that I am eternally grateful to God. He is not only Savior and Redeemer, but He is also Helper, Friend, and Connector of all the pieces and all the people.

An extra shout out is entirely essential to Sarah Baughman, my writing partner, friend, and editor of this text. This book would not be in print without her help and expertise; also to Melissa of Melissa Sue Photo and Design for the cover design, as well as the internal design elements. Melissa's designs always bring color and life to my black and white words and I stand amazed at the results. Finally, one day I sat in a small church in Ohio and heard God say He loved me and this study was born. Without Jesus where would I be? Thank you, to the One whom my soul loves.